BASIC ATTENDING SKILLS

(THIRD EDITION)

Allen E. Ivey, Norma Gluckstern,

and Mary Bradford Ivey

MICROTRAINING ASSOCIATES

Dedication

To: *Bill and John Ivey*

Amie Gluckstern

Elizabeth and Kathryn Bohn

Each of you has contributed in a special way to the development of microcounseling. Your participation, encouragement, and challenges have been part of Microtraining's growth.

Permission to paraphrase certain portions of this book have been granted by Charles C Thomas Publishers, Springfield, Illinois. Videotapes to accompany this book are available from Microtraining Associates, Inc.

CONTENTS

Basic Attending Skills in Brief Summary Statements

The first task in a helping relationship is to listen.

The second task is to listen with individual and multicultural sensitivity.

CHAPTER 1

BASIC ATTENDING SKILLS: AN OVERVIEW

Listening to another person and giving them your full attention is one of the greatest gifts you can give. We grow in relationship to others and the foundation of relationship is your ability to listen and indicate your caring. Interviewing, counseling, and therapy—the helping arts—are all founded on effective listening.

Before we start, take just a moment and think back on a time when someone listened to you in a helpful way. If you can, get an image of that situation and recall what you saw, heard, and felt. And, as you recall that helpful time, reflect on what that person did to be helpful. This may help you connect personally with the power and utility of listening. Use the following lines for your recollections.

How did it feel to have someone truly listen? _____

_____

What specifically did the listener *do* which helped? _____

_____

Your personal experience with being listened to (or being failed to be listened to) may be part of the reason you are working with this book. As you begin, recall your own powerful experiences with those who listen and those who fail to listen. Your own experience can serve as a meaningful supplement to the fundamentals of listening stressed in these pages.

This book, *Basic Attending Skills,* will provide you with a fundamental understanding and competence in the most important skills of helping, counseling, and therapy. These listening skills will help you make contact with your clients and to hear how they understand the world. In addition, these skills are basic to empathy, the ability to experience life through another person's eyes, ears, and feelings.

Many of us tend to give advice and suggestions when someone comes for help. However, we may be disappointed and surprised when our good ideas are sometimes ignored. It is important to remember that clients usually have problems that took *time* to develop. Doesn't it make good sense just to stop for a while and hear clients out fully before you move to suggesting what can be done? You will find that waiting and first listening to your client will help you understand what really needs to be done.

The central maxim of *Basic Attending Skills* is:

> *Listen, listen, listen, then listen some more*
> *before taking action or giving advice.*

If you listen to and attend to your clients, many times they can resolve issues on their own. This book stresses client growth potential. Listening to clients and enabling them to find their strength is basic to the helping process.

HOW WILL YOU LEARN *BASIC ATTENDING SKILLS*?

Twenty-five years of clinical experience and empirical research on the interviewing process in microcounseling underlie the ideas presented here. Microcounseling breaks down the complex interview into component parts and teaches them one at a time. The advantage of this process is that you can readily master specific techniques and strategies that will make a difference in the lives of those with whom you work.

The microcounseling training system consists of the following steps:

1. *Introduction/Warm-up.* You will receive a brief introduction to a basic skill of interviewing. Important interviewing issues relating to the skill are summarized.

2. *Reading about the skill.* A brief summary describes the key components of the interviewing skill you are about to learn.

3. *Seeing a model of the skill in action.* Seeing a person perform a helping skill can bring reading and theory into real life. Videotape models provide one

way to see a skill in action. In addition, this book provides example transcripts of interviews illustrating the ideas in action.

4. *Practice.* Perhaps even more important than watching others is you taking time to practice the skills in each session. Practicing and testing the specific skills will help you take theory directly into practice. With some more complex skills, you may need more than one practice session.

5. *Generalization.* Specific suggestions for taking the concepts of the training session to your home setting are included with each skill.

The first three steps focus on you learning the skill and should lead you to an understanding of why this particular skill is important and what it can do for you and your client. The last two steps, however, are the critical ones. There are many people who can develop an intellectual understanding of the helping process—but understanding is not competence in the interview.

The competent, effective interviewer practices the skills to a level of mastery and is able to take the ideas of the skill "home" to his or her daily life and work setting.

WHAT IS THE TRAINING OUTLINE AND SEQUENCE?

There are six major skill areas in this program. A brief definition of each and its major function in the interview follows:

Skill Area	Definition and Interview Function
Attending Behavior	Individually and culturally appropriate verbal and nonverbal behavior in the interview is central to the helping process. This demonstrates that you are listening and encourages the client to talk more freely.
Open Invitation to Talk	Open questions help the client explore issues and talk at greater length. Closed questions lead to focused answers, usually relatively short.
Clarifying —Encourage —Paraphrase	Encourages are brief responses such as head nods, "uh-huh," and single words or phrases. They encourage client exploration in more depth. The paraphrase feeds back

to the client the essence of what has been said. It thus provides a check on the accuracy of your listening and may enable the client to move on to a new topic.

Reflecting Feelings

Reflection of feeling identifies and feeds back to the helpee her or his underlying emotional experience. Exploration of emotion is basic to helping and client decision making and action.

Summarization

This skill enables you to feed back to the client the essence of longer statements describing behavior, thought, and emotion. The skill is useful in clarifying what has happened in key interview segments and in beginning and ending the interview.

Integration of Skills
—Five Interview Stages

The final segment of this program brings together the several skills above into a well-formed interview. You will find it is possible to conduct a full interview using only listening skills. Five specific stages of the interview are defined.

These several skills are termed the *basic listening sequence.* Observation and research have revealed that effective counselors are not the only ones who use these skills. The competent physician must listen to the patient before providing a diagnosis. The manager must listen to staff and learn important facts before making an important decision.

You will find that the basic listening sequence taught in this book is critical in many different situations. If you listen carefully, you will find that answers often flow easily from those whom you will help. If your clients don't come up with their own answers, you at least have an information base that can help you act more effectively.

Once you have studied and mastered each one of the basic listening skills above, this book provides advanced instruction that can enable you to adapt the skills in a variety of situations. Drawing out client behaviors, thoughts, and feelings is central to this process.

As you listen, there is a style of positive interviewing and listening which tends to be more effective, regardless of your work setting. The positive asset search is discussed in the following section.

ACCENTUATE THE POSITIVE (BUT BE AWARE OF THE NEGATIVE)

Beginning helpers occasionally have the tendency to become fascinated with "war stories," the basic facts about someone else's problems and concerns. Their questions, comments, and attention focus on negative things about the helpee. It is fascinating to learn the intimate facts of someone else's life. Helping is not about prying into other people's affairs.

If you focus on "war stories," the helpee frequently jumps into your trap with glee, delighted that someone is finally listening. A possible result of the naive helper's need to pry into another person's life *and* the helpee's need to share how "bad" the world is may be a spiral that defines the situation as worse than it really is.

At the other extreme, some beginning helpers are so anxious that they reassure clients before they have listened to the full story of the concern. The rescuer is perhaps even more dangerous than the prying, probing helper. Many professionals and volunteer helpers are so eager to aid clients facing difficult issues that they gloss over and hide issues so the helpee "doesn't feel bad." Watch out for rescuing!

People talk about what other people will listen to. If a beginning counselor or helper only listens to weaknesses and problems, the client/helpee will only talk about weaknesses and problems. While airing of concerns is helpful and often necessary, it is only part of anyone's life picture. On the other hand, if the helper avoids hard issues, so does the helpee.

Another basic maxim of the helping process:

> *Helpees will talk about topics to which*
> *you are able and willing to listen.*
> *However, avoid prying and rescuing.*

Thus we believe a certain portion of any session held by beginning helpers should focus on strengths and capacities of the helpee to cope successfully with the world. This means listening for positive as well as negative comments. For example:

Helpee:	I really feel mixed-up and confused, nothing is going right. Society is all screwed up, the rich get richer and the poor get poorer. I worked hard, but I still get laid off.
Helper:	(Accentuating the negative) Society is really grim, you feel really hopeless. What are some other things that bother you?
Helper:	(Accentuating the positive) Losing your job at a time like this is really hard. I hear you say you did good work. Could you share some specific things you did on your job that you were particularly proud of?
Helper:	(Too positive) Not to worry—it's always darkest before the dawn. (Rescuing) Let me do the worrying for a while. We'll find a way. What do you want me to do for you first?

The first response does acknowledge the feelings of desperation and hopelessness of the helpee and may be a satisfactory response in a larger context. However, there are would-be helpers who only reinforce negative self-comments and troubles. The second response acknowledges the feelings, but also emphasizes the positive aspects of the situation, aiding the helpee in sorting out positive resources. The third response (reassurance) is often helpful, but can be overdone. This response fails to acknowledge the helpee's hurt and the helper has taken on responsibility too soon for solving the client's difficulties.

Another critical maxim of *Basic Attending Skills:*

Focus on the positive—
search for positive assets in the client and the client's situation.

KEYS FOR EFFECTIVE HELPING: RESPECT YOURSELF AND THE CLIENT

The program you are entering is highly skill oriented. We have noted that some beginning helpers get worried about what they "should" be doing when relating to a helpee. They get so worried about doing the "right" thing that in the process they become confused and less effective. It is important that you generate a solid theory and philosophy of helping. Two key suggestions leading toward effective philosophy and theory follow.

The first step toward effective helping is the most important—*respect and have confidence in yourself!* Unless you are comfortable with yourself, you won't be able to help others.

Each of us ultimately must define our own style of helping. When a skill appeals to you, go ahead and try it . . . but always be sure that it feels right to you. On the other hand, if that skill or concept doesn't appeal to you, it is still probably a good idea to try it and check it out thoroughly. But if you find it doesn't "fit," it is best to acknowledge that fact and stay with a style which is more natural to you.

Another important maxim:

> *As a helper, you can be mostly helpful if you are truly yourself.*
> *Seek to define your own style of helping.*

The second suggestion relating to a basic philosophy of helping comes from the basic skill orientation of this book. We ourselves have found that most confusion around interviewing disappears if we are willing to listen carefully and attend to others. When you find yourself confused, lost or wondering what to do in the interview—listen and use the attending skills of this book.

This book focuses on listening to the client. If respecting yourself is half the battle, the other half is likely *respect thy neighbor—the client.* One effective way to honor others is to listen and attend to what they are telling you carefully and respectfully.

ARE YOU WILLING TO LISTEN AND TO LEARN FROM THE CLIENT?

The major temptation in helping is to attempt to solve the problem of the helpee as soon as possible. The beginning helper often barely gives the helpee time to get the problem out before starting to offer sympathy and solutions.

We urge you to stay away from giving answers to those whom you would help throughout the skill sessions of this program. Your task is to be a good listener, to demonstrate quality attending skills. The use of advice, interpretation, or suggestions is for a later, more advanced, state of helping. *Your job is to listen.* Very few people in our society are effective listeners. It seems sad that we must teach people to listen, but it is a necessary skill that our culture does not emphasize.

It may be hard for you to listen and stop talking. Even more difficult may be working with microcounseling single skills. You'll want to jump around to many different skills. Staying with the single skill of paraphrasing, for example, may be hard work and seem unnatural. However, effective paraphrasing is a difficult skill and unless you are willing to feel uncomfortable at first, it is a skill you may never master.

The ideas in this book in one sense are simple and clear. Clarity does not mean that practice is not necessary. Just because you can understand the basics of attending does not mean you can use the ideas when faced with a difficult and challenging client. Even the most experienced professional can benefit from more careful attention to the language and world of the client.

A crucial question to ask yourself is whether or not you are willing to do the work to become the most effective listener possible. Practice is essential for mastery. Providing suggestions and "answers" is easy; effective listening demands more effort.

BASIC ATTENDING SKILLS, CULTURAL EMPATHY, AND BASIC TRUST

Empathy asks you to hear and sense the experiential world of another person accurately. We talk about seeing the world as the other person sees, hearing what they hear, and feeling what they feel. Empathy requires the ability to suspend your own thoughts and feelings and to enter into the world of another.

Cultural empathy extends empathy to another level. We live in a multicultural, pluralistic world. The importance of listening skills becomes amplified when we look at culturally different groups. North Americans of European, Latin, Asian, and African extraction represent culturally different backgrounds. Their individual and group communication styles differ.

Men and women at times represent different cultures. Research reveals that women tend to listen more effectively than men. Women tend to be more active listeners and demonstrate this through both verbal and nonverbal listening skills.

However, men too can listen effectively, but for many men, listening will take more work and effort.

Regardless of gender or cultural background, entering into another person's world empathically is facilitated through the attending skills discussed in this book. This means you have a responsibility to listen and observe. Developing *basic trust* and a good relationship are essential.

Basic trust and a "good relationship" are not easily defined. It is here that we ask you to turn to yourself, your good will, and your interest in people. You will find that each individual, regardless of cultural background, has a personal style. Some will want to share themselves with you immediately while others will be more hesitant—you'll sense the openness of your client early in the session. With the client who is ready to talk, the listening skills presented here can be used immediately. With others, you will want to spend time developing a relationship of trust before you seek to help them with their concerns.

The routes toward basic trust are many and will depend on you and the client. During this process of trust building, you will find awareness of attending behavior (next chapter) and the listening skills is vital and important in the relationship that evolves.

> *Earn trust so that you may listen effectively.*

We are often asked if microcounseling is a theory and mode of helping in itself or if it is merely a set of practical skills. We believe that the ideas and skills presented here are both theoretically significant and practical. Microcounseling was first developed as a set of skills for use with other theories. However, regardless of the theory you select, you will find that the listening skills here are invaluable in being an effective helper, counselor, or therapist.

> *Attending and listening at times may be sufficient*
> *for effective helping, counseling, and psychotherapy.*

Basic Attending Skills are foundational to the helping process. A second series, *Basic Influencing Skills,* focuses on using your ability to produce change. Some other readings on microskills follow.

SUGGESTED FURTHER READINGS AND VIDEOTAPES

Ivey, A. & Gluckstern, N. *Basic Influencing Skills.* North Amherst, Massachusetts: Microtraining, 1984.
This book, and accompanying videotape series is a follow-up program to *Basic Attending Skills.* Skills such as interpretation, self-disclosure, and assertiveness training are emphasized in this advanced series. In addition, brief workshop sessions around empathic dimensions such as concreteness, immediacy, and confrontation elaborate ideas expressed here.

Materials to Support Training in Multicultural Counseling

Sue, D. *Barriers to Cross-Cultural Counseling, Cultural Identity Development, and Culture Specific Strategies in Counseling.* North Amherst, Ma: Microtraining, 1990, 1991.
Three videotapes which present specifics of multicultural counseling and therapy. *Culture-Specific Strategies* is a particularly powerful and useful videotape that may be used to accompany training in *Basic Attending Skills.*

Sue, D., & Sue, D. *Counseling the Culturally Different.* New York: Wiley, 1990.
The standard of the field. An excellent source of specifics for working with culturally different clients.

Additional Books and Material on the Microskills Framework

Ivey. A. *Intentional Interviewing and Counseling.* (Second Edition) Pacific Grove, Ca.: Brooks/Cole, 1988.
An overview of the interview and the skills of helping. Special attention is given to skill sequencing, developing a treatment plan, and proper selection of skills.

Evans, D. Hearn, M., Uhlemann, M., and Ivey, A. *Essential Interviewing: A programmed Approach to Effective Communication.* (Third Edition) Pacific Grove, Ca.: Brooks/Cole, 1992.
A programmed text elaborating on microskill concepts.

Ivey, A. *Microcounseling: Innovations in Interviewing.* Springfield, Ill.: Thomas, 1971.
The original microcounseling description. In the two editions, this is the second most cited book in counseling during the past decade.

Ivey, A. and Authier, J. *Microcounseling: Innovations in Interviewing, Counseling, Psychotherapy, and Psychoeducation.* (Second edition) Springfield, Ill.: Thomas, 1978. Approximately double the size of the original microcounseling text, this book updates research and clinical practice and discusses over 150 data-based studies on the microcounseling model. In addition, over 15 research instruments are included in the book.

Ivey, A. *Managing Face to Face Communication: Survival Tactics for People and Products in the 1990's.* Lund, Sweden: Chartwell-Bratt, 1988. (Available from Microtraining Associates, Inc.) Application of attending and influencing skills in business. Videotapes for management education available.

Ivey, A., Ivey, M., and Simek-Downing, L. *Counseling and Psychotherapy: Multicultural Perspectives* (3rd Edition) Boston: Allyn & Bacon, 1993. Introductory text based on the microskills model which includes information on how the skills are sequenced and used in varying psychological theories. Includes a major emphasis on counseling multicultural populations.

Two books which apply microtraining concepts to developmental processes may also be of interest to you:

Ivey, A. *Developmental Therapy: Theory into Practice.* San Francisco: Jossey-Bass, 1986. Theory and practice illustrating how to integrate a new reading of Piagetian theory into the helping process.

Ivey, A. *Developmental Strategies for Helpers Individual, Family and Network Interventions.* Pacific Grove, Ca.: Brooks/Cole, 1991. Applications of developmental theory to counseling and therapy process. Extensive emphasis on transcripts, clinical applications, and multicultural issues.

Microcounseling books or videotapes are currently available in Chinese, Danish, Dutch, French, German, Greek, Indonesian, Japanese, Norwegian, and Swedish. A "British-English" version a now available. Write Microtraining Associates, Box 641, North Amherst, Massachusetts, 01059 for information.

*Attending behaviors are different
in different cultures.*

*There are many effective ways to
listen to another individual.*

CHAPTER 2

ATTENDING BEHAVIOR:
THE FOUNDATION OF EFFECTIVE LISTENING

The first thing that the helper must learn is to *listen* to the helpee. But what is listening? We all know what it is, but defining the term precisely is another matter. The central goal of this first session in microtraining is to help you identify specifically what listening is and to consider the many implications of this definition.

The exercises and readings in this chapter seek to help you:

1. Understand the importance of effective listening.

2. Define four central dimensions of attending behavior and identify some critical individual and cultural differences underlying effective attending.

3. Understand the critical concept of selective attention. Clients will tend to talk about topics to which you are willing to listen.

4. Demonstrate attending behavior yourself in a practice individual interview. You are also encouraged to practice these concepts in a group session.

5. Use attending behavior in your daily life and also to consider how you might teach the skill to others.

WHAT LISTENING IS *NOT!*

One effective way to discover the nature of listening is through examining what it is *not.* Find another person and go through the following exercise or watch the behavior of another pair:

> Person 1   is to be the interviewer/helper. However, the task is to do the *worst* job of listening possible. It helps to exaggerate. You may also want to think of an individual who talked to you in real life and did a very poor job of hearing what you had to say.

Person 2   is to be the client/helpee. Regardless of how poorly the interviewer behaves, your task is to keep talking.

Suggested topics for the brief two-minute role-play are: a job interview, a discussion of a family conflict, choice of courses, or a topic of mutual interest to the helper and the helpee.

List below your observations of what helping/counseling isn't. After you make your list, check to see if what your list represents is observable behavior, something that you can see (e.g., the helper may appear anxious—true, but what do you *see* that makes you think he/she is anxious? Wringing the hands, sitting tensely, stammering?).

Specific observable behaviors which represent ineffective listening:

_____

_____

_____

After discussions with others and obtaining reactions from the helpee, you may want to add to the above list. As a final step, look over the list and note the things which you think most important. Underline those you would stress if you were teaching basic helping skills. In the following reading, you'll see what research and practice have found to be most basic. However, it is also important to remember your own list for it is uniquely yours and provides some important clues as to your own approach to analyzing and teaching the interview.

The following *Basic Skill* description lays a foundation for becoming a helper. The behaviors described are bedrocks for effective listening. Without the following skills, even the most brilliant helper may fail.

ATTENDING BEHAVIOR: BASIC SKILL #1

The most basic skill of helping is listening to those whom you attempt to help. But what is listening? We use the term "attending behavior" to remind us that listening consists of specific and observable dimensions. Attending behavior is a basic, rather simple skill—but with many, many profound implications.

Four key dimensions comprise attending behavior:

1. *Eye contact.* If you are going to talk to someone, look at him or her. No need to stare, just be aware that you are talking to another person. You'll also want to notice *eye contact breaks.*. When you look away you are sometimes telling the person you are working with that you aren't really attending (but don't stare—some natural breaks do occur). Later on, you'll start noticing that eye contact breaks on the part of helpees give you clues as to where that person "is at." More on that later.

2. *Attentive body language.* We usually think that counseling is a verbal relationship. In truth, some estimates say that 85% of our communication is nonverbal. Think for a minute—how does your body communicate that it is listening? Find your own natural listening style and check with others to see how it "comes across." The basic attentive listening posture in our culture is a slight forward trunk lean with a relaxed easy posture. But find your own style—if you are not true to yourself, you won't appear attentive to your client.

    Later on you'll want to start looking for small signs of tension (frowns, tense mouth or chin, clenched fists, marked shifts in body posture at key times in the interview) in both yourself and the client. But for now, simply assume a relaxed body position and communicate that you are involved. Your awareness of body language will naturally increase throughout this training series.

3. *Vocal style.* Changes in speech rate, volume, and tone often indicate interest or disinterest. Speech hesitations or stammers often occur at tension points. The music of emotion and feeling is often most apparent through the voice.

4.   *Verbal following.* A frequent basic question of beginning helpers is "What do I say?" We say, *relax*—it doesn't help to be nervous. When in doubt as to what to say, take whatever the helpee has said and respond to it in a natural way. Direct whatever you may say to what the helpee has just said or perhaps said earlier in your session. *The helper seldom needs to introduce a new topic.*

Your prime task is simply to stay with what has already been said. In summary, don't topic jump!

Cultural differences. It is critical that you remember that the attending behavior of different cultural and ethnic groups varies in style. Eye contact among some Southwest Native Americans may represent a hostile act, the physical distance between two speakers may vary from culture to culture (e.g., people from the Middle East stand much more closely together than middle-class people in the U.S.) and the standard vocal tone of American English may be slow and boring to some Latina/o peoples. Attending behavior appears to be a universal cultural phenomena. However, attending skills manifest themselves differently among different people.

The following chart summarizes only some key differences in listening skills among different groups. And, as you read the following, recall that individual differences within a group vary extensively. Avoid stereotyping your client.

Eye Contact   African-Americans, Latina/o, and Native Americans may avoid eye contact as a sign of respect. With Latina/o's, direct sustained eye contact can represent a challenge to authority. A bowed head may be a sign of respect from Native Americans.

Body Language   African-Americans may have public behavior which seems emotionally intense and demonstrative to European-Americans. A slap on the back may be insulting to an Asian-American or Latina/o.

Vocal Style   Latina/o's often begin meetings with lengthy greetings and pleasant talk before getting down to key issues.

European-Americans tend to value quiet, controlled vocal style which other groups may see as manipulative and/or cold.

Verbal following   Asian-Americans may prefer a more indirect and subtle communication and consider the African-American or European-American styles too direct and confrontational. Personal questions may be especially offensive to Native Americans.

Individual differences. Similarly, individual helpees vary in their attending patterns. A depressed client will have difficulty in maintaining eye contact with you at all and likely have one topic—how bad things are. A client talking about an embarrassing or difficult issue may avoid eye contact and topic jump. When one combines individual and cultural variation, it is obvious that this most basic skill of listening can become very complex.

Thus it is suggested that not only do you demonstrate attending behavior yourself, but that you also *observe the attending patterns of others.* You may find that what seems to be rude or distant behavior is simply culturally appropriate patterns on the part of the other person and your own style may be interpreted by the client as even more rude. And, as your observation skills increase, you will note vast individual differences in patterns of attention on the part of your helpees, regardless of culture. Attending behavior provides a framework for observing your own behavior and the behavior of your clients.

Summary. In briefer form, your goal in interviewing is to be a good listener through the use of specific, observable behaviors which are culturally appropriate:

1. Use varied eye contact to communicate with the helpee. Be aware that different cultural groups may have varying patterns of eye contact.

2. Maintain an attentive body posture using a natural *relaxed* posture and gestures. Use your body to communicate your involvement.

3. Use a natural vocal style. Your voice communicates your emotions.

4. Stay on the topic. Don't topic jump or interrupt. Simply note what the helpee has said and take your cues from him/her. There is no need to go into your own head to think of what to say. The helpee has already told you.

If you get confused and can't think of anything to say, simply hesitate a moment and think back to something said earlier that interested you. Make a comment or ask a question about that topic. You are still attending! This simple point is a lifesaver for both beginning helpers and highly experienced professionals.

WHERE DO YOU FOCUS YOUR ATTENTION?

The purpose here is to summarize some further implications of attending behavior with special reference to individual helper "style." The essential point of this manual is summarized below:

Helpee's talk about what helpers listen to. At first glance attending and attending skills impress the beginner as "non-directive" in nature. Attending skills lead as much as they follow.

For example, a client may say "I'm doing really poor work in school this past month. I'm really uptight right now. Things are going bad at home—Mom and Dad are talking divorce." Before going further, write below what you might say to this client.

I would say_____

_____

Compare your responses with the five following possibilities below which all attend to the client in some way:

1. "In what subjects are you having the most problems?"

2. "You're tense right now."

3. "Sounds like right now you're really concerned about what your parents fighting means for you?"

4.   "What specifically is going on at home?"

5.   "What type of work does your Dad do?"

The response selected by the helper often says more about the helper than it does about the helpee. Notice what topics you selectively attend to. What topics turn you on, turn you off? What do you zero in on? What do you avoid?

In the example above, the first response above focuses on schoolwork, the next two on the feelings of the client in the interview, the last two on the family context. All of the responses are attending and potentially helpful, but each response focuses on the problem from a different vantage point.

It is important to note the topics to which you attend and those which you tend to ignore. In the example above, schoolwork, the helpee's personal feelings, and the family context are all important. Nonetheless, most experts believe it is most important to focus on the feelings and thoughts of the client sitting there in front of you (#2 and #3 above). Was your first focus on the client, the school problem, the family, or some other issue?

The three aspects of attending behavior provide you with important cues as to what your "style" is. For example, where do you break eye contact? Do you unconsciously avert your eyes when someone talks about religion, thereby indicating this is a topic you don't care to hear about? Do your eyes brighten when the helpee talks about sex and you find that all your helpees are talking about this area? Careful examination of videotapes will reveal clear points where you reinforce certain helpee comments and extinguish others.

Similarly, note your pattern of body language in relation to specific topics. When do you sit forward, move back, tighten a fist, or relax? What does your body language communicate to your helpee? You'll find your body often mirrors that of your client if you are truly listening. This is termed "movement synchrony" and is a variable which can only really be studied by videotape.

The examples above illustrate the importance of selective attention in verbal following. *Once again, helpees talk about topics which you are willing and able to listen to.*

Constantly monitor your patterns of selective attention both verbally and nonverbally. It will give you a clue as to your natural "style." Finally, note your "percent of talk-time." Some helpers talk too much. Attending is about listening. Do you give your helpee enough "air-time" on topics of interest to her or him? Audio or videorecord a practice session and note how much you talk and how much the client talks in a session. Use your watch or a stop watch and check it out.

USING ATTENDING BEHAVIOR SKILLS WITH FAMILIES AND GROUPS

Increasingly, helpers are being called on to work with groups and families. Attending behavior skills are just as important in these settings as with an individual. Most helpers learn individual interviewing first. Individual work focuses on the single helpee. Frequently, beginning family and groupworkers focus solely on individuals and their problems, ignoring the potential power of the group.

As you work with the skills in this book, pause frequently to recall that the same skills are useful in family and group work. Following are some important issues in using attending beyond individual interviewing.

Do you balance your attending? Do you look at all group and family members or are there some few individuals who have the vast majority of your attention? Many helpers who move from individual work to family work falter when they give one or two people their primary attention. Some helpers give more attention to women in families, others to men. Some totally ignore children in family groups.

What are the attending behavior patterns in the group or family? You will find that certain members of the family or group are sought for leadership, particularly on certain topics. You will find that people who tend to have alliances in the family or group have similar patterns of body posture and may mirror one another. Those who are in conflict in the group will tend to avert eye contact and show signs of bodily tension.

Constantly practice your observations of nonverbal behavior. You will find that family and group members respond differently to you personally. These data can be a clue to your own effectiveness and may even give you information as to culturally appropriate behavior if the group or family comes from a different background than you.

Are there multicultural issues in the group? Again, recall that multicultural issues are critical in the helping process. You will want to learn specifics of the cultural group with whom you are working. Not only is it possible that their patterns of eye contact and body language are different from your own, but who talks after whom can be important. In some cultures, the father is expected to speak for the family as a whole while with others the situation may be very different.

Working in a multicultural setting such as Canada or the U.S. provides helpers with the opportunity for a lifetime of learning about differences in attending styles. Groupwork with those from the Canadian Atlantic Provinces, California, and the Southern States varies. Men and women's groups have different styles, just as African-American, Latino, and White groups will vary.

Can you attend to the family or group as a whole. Essentially, learn to focus your attention on the entire "family" or "group." Deliberately use statements which contain the words "family" and "group"—"This group/family seems to feel anxious about meeting together." "The group/family seems to be good at supporting each other."

One general rule for family and groupwork is that one-third of the time should be spent on the total process of the group (with a focus on the words "family" and "group"); one-third of the time should be spent on individuals in the group and their behavior, thoughts, and feelings; and one-third of the time on the group's special topic or problem.

Thus, if you are working with a group of teens who come from alcoholic families, you will want to balance your attention to the three topics. Equal time and attention can be given to the general problem of alcoholism and the family, the individual problems of the teens, and to the group process itself.

PRACTICING ATTENDING BEHAVIOR

You have now seen negative examples of attending behavior and read about the possibilities inherent in the concepts. Hopefully, you will have had the opportunity to view a live demonstration, film, or videotape of the skill in action. But what is most important is your ability to engage in attending skills. The following is suggested to practice attending behavior.

1. *Develop a working group.* You can't practice attending behavior alone. The most effective group size is three or four. However, two people can be sufficient for practice.

2. *Assign roles for the first practice session.* The following are listed in order of critical importance:

   a. *Helper.* This individual practices attending behavior in a short role-play.

   b. *Helpee.* This person serves as client and discusses real or role-played concerns. The helpee also provides feedback to the helper after the role-play.

   c. *Observer/operator.* This person operates the videotape or audiotape equipment and provides verbal and written feedback to the helper. If no equipment is available, the emphasis is solely on observation.

   d. *Second observer.* This individual provides written feedback to the helper and ideally concentrates observations on nonverbal dimensions which may be missed by others. This is especially important if no videotape is available for practice.

3. *Determine topic for role-play.* The helpee decides what he or she would like to talk about in the brief role-play. While any topic may be suitable, we suggest that you use past and present vocational interests and jobs. The task of the helper is to enable the helpee to talk freely. As you gain more experience with the skills, select increasingly challenging topics. Attitudes or experiences with alcohol and drugs is a very useful topic which virtually all helpers will encounter.

4. *Watch time carefully and provide feedback.* The role-play should be approximately 3-4 minutes in length and video or audiorecorded. If not

recorded, the observers become especially important to provide feedback. Use the feedback sheets provided and give specific information to the helpee. Do not be judgmental (e.g., "That was a great job!"). Rather, attempt to be specific and concrete (e.g., "You maintained eye contact and the client responded with a gradually relaxing body posture and vocal tone.").

5. *Rotate roles* so that every person has an opportunity to serve as helper and helpee. Again, remember to divide time for practice equally.

GROUP/FAMILY PRACTICE IN ATTENDING BEHAVIOR

BASIC ATTENDING SKILLS does not claim to make you an expert group or family interviewer or counselor. However, whether you are a beginner or even an advanced expert, some time spent deliberately working with the skills of this book can make you more effective with groups and families.

1. *Develop a working group.* For practice, a working group of four is recommended, a facilitator and three group members.

2. *If possible, assign two additional roles for the practice session.*

   a. *Observer/operator.* This person operates the videotape or audiotape equipment and provides verbal and written feedback to the group. If no equipment is available, the emphasis is solely on observation.

   b. *Second observer.* This individual provides written feedback to the helper and ideally concentrates observations on nonverbal dimensions which may be missed by others.

3. *Determine topic for role-play.* A useful and stimulating topic for the group can be taken from the alcohol and drug area—a working topic might be "the meaning of alcohol," but the specific topic should be decided on by the group and its leader.

4. *Planning.* Divide the time between the topic (alcohol suggested in this case), the individuals in the group (their feelings and attitudes toward alcohol), and the group itself (how the group interacts as a whole). For this first practice

exercise, follow time guidelines carefully. In the beginnings of family and groupwork, you will find that a firm structure is useful and helps make the group or family sense themselves as a "group" rather than just a collection of individuals.

5. *Watch time carefully and provide feedback.* The role-play group session should be approximately 30 minutes in length and video or audiorecorded. If not recorded, the observers become especially important to provide feedback. Complete the feedback sheets provided and give specific information to the helpee.

RATING AND BEHAVIORAL COUNT SHEET FOR ATTENDING BEHAVIOR

Check or rate the following specific dimensions of attending on the part of the helper.

1. *Attending Behavior Counts*

	Ineffective Modeling Tape	*Effective Modeling Tape*	*(Use Extra Space for Other Ratings You May Use in This Workshop)*
No. of Inappropriate Eye Contact Breaks			
No. of Extraneous Unnatural Movements			
No. of Vocal Style Distractions			
No. of Topic Jumps			
Total Non-Attending			

2. *Patterns of Attending Behavior.* Are there certain topics on which the helper seems to demonstrate more extensive attending behavior? Are there places where the helper seems to lessen attending behavior and avoid a topic?

_____

_____

_____

_____

3. *Observations of Helpee Behavior.* What do you observe in terms of the helpee's reactions verbally and nonverbally to the interview? Did the helpee have sufficient "airtime"? Use a stop watch and calculate percent of talk time for helper and client.

_____

_____

_____

_____

4. *Cite one specific strength you saw in this interview.*

_____

_____

_____

_____

5. *Cite one specific thing which the helper might want to add to make the interview more effective.*

_____

_____

_____

_____

DO-USE-TEACH CONTRACT

You first had an opportunity to understand what the concept of attending behavior was about. You then experienced the ideas of attending behavior first hand. Now is the time to decide what these concepts mean to you and how they can be used in your own life space.

We know from past work that the concepts when taught are often useful. We find ourselves concerned that they are not used as widely in as many different settings as possible. What we'd like you to do now is think about how you might *use* the concepts of attending behavior outside the interview.

Ways that people have used attending behavior in their own lives include:

> A beginning helper tried it with a helpee when she didn't know what to do. It works!

> A shy person who couldn't talk to anyone tried attending and found it provided an opening wedge in conversation.

> A man in trouble with his boss tried deliberate attending and discovered he was missing some crucial messages.

> At the family dinner table, a husband and wife found they weren't listening to their children and then used attending to open up the family interaction.

> A depressed individual found that going out and deliberately attending to someone else helped him get out of himself. We have found that attending skills are particularly useful in work with clients who show slight, moderate, or severe depression.

> A student deliberately attended to her teacher and, to her surprise, found the teacher talking to her and no one else!

Personal experience with using attending is crucial. Our helping skills should not be just used in the interview; they have meaning in our daily lives as well.

What do you want to do to test out the value of attending in your own life? Write a specific plan and outline in detail how you will make the concepts relevant to you.

My plan to use attending behavior in my own life is _____

_____

_____

_____

Talk with someone about your plan to use attending. Is it specific enough? Will it work? Can you arrange a time to get together with this individual to report how your contract worked out?

TEACH

Next, we would like you to think about someone or some group with whom you might like to test your understanding and facility with attending behavior by teaching them what you have learned in this chapter.

Teaching someone else about attending behavior has taken many forms:

• Using this same workshop format to teach teachers, parents, peer facilitators, hot-line operators, etc., these same listening skills which you have learned.

• Labeling listening skills in your own way. After all, you don't have to use the terms eye contact, body language, and verbal following. Some might prefer very different use of words.

• If you are helping someone in a counseling session, try teaching these basic skills. Teaching attending is especially helpful to depressed individuals or those with weak social and interpersonal skills. When clients attend to someone else, they are not attending to their own difficulties.

Teaching your clients listening skills can be very helpful. For some clients, learning how to listen may be more important than traditional counseling. To whom and when would you like to teach attending behavior? And how would you do it? Write a contract with someone in the group to actually set up a teaching plan.

DO—USE—TEACH

You don't know what you are doing until you can teach it to someone else.

*An open invitation to talk is a gift
to the client.*

*But, sometimes that gift of
questioning becomes "grilling" and
may be intrusive.*

*How are you going to find a
balance?*

CHAPTER 3

OPEN INVITATION TO TALK

Questions help an interview move along. They open new areas for discussion, they assist in pinpointing issues, they can be used to facilitate helpee self-exploration. In recent years, questioning approaches to counseling and therapy have gained increased favor. Many cognitive counselors or family therapists, for example, may use as much as fifty per cent questioning in their sessions. At the same time, it must be remembered that a few practitioners have suggested that the helper should *never* ask questions. One of your central tasks in this session will be to define where you stand on the use of questions.

The exercises and readings in this chapter seek to help you:

1. Develop awareness of both strengths and weaknesses of questioning skills. You will be asked to generate your own position on the use of questions in the interview.

2. Define the difference between open and closed questions.

3. Identify how different question stems ("Could," "What," "How," and "Why") tend to lead to varying types of client talk.

4. Demonstrate the skills of question asking in a practice interview. You are also encouraged to test these skills in practice with couples, groups, and family.

5. Use questioning skills in your daily life and to consider how you might teach the skills to others, including your clients.

WHAT ARE YOUR FEELINGS AND EXPERIENCES WITH QUESTIONS?

In North American society, questions come endlessly. Children ask us questions almost as their first sentences, teachers question us in school, our employers question our performance and skills, and in the evening we watch television entertainers use questions to bring out their guests. Clearly, questions are an important part of our culture.

Questions also indicate that a person is interested in you and what you have to say. Good questions help people explore themselves and their feelings more deeply.

Yet, questions have varying impact on different people. Some feel put "on the spot" or "grilled" when someone asks them questions. If you have not established a solid base of trust with another person or a client, questions used too early can interfere with the development of rapport. This is particularly true with clients who are culturally different from you.

Take some time to note both your positive and negative experiences with questions below. Has you personal experience of questions been mainly positive or negative?

My personal experience with questions has been:

Positives: _____

_____

_____

_____

Negatives: _____

_____

_____

_____

The position taken in this book is that questions are a helpful and necessary part of most interviews, but that we all must be aware of their limitations. Skilled question asking can result in clients learning how to question and examine themselves. Let us now consider more information about the critical skills of questioning.

OPEN INVITATION TO TALK: BASIC SKILL #2

The client comes into an interview with a concern or problem. The initial task of the interviewer is to stay out of the client's way so as to find out how the client sees the situation and defines the issues. Most useful in this process is the technique of providing limited structure through the use of an open invitation to talk.

Compare the following examples:

> Open: Could you tell me a little bit about your marriage? How are things with your husband/wife?

> Closed: Are you married? Do you get along with your wife/husband?

It may be observed that the open questions provide room for the client to express the real self without the imposed categories of the helper. An open comment allows the client an opportunity to explore self and situation.

Closed questions, on the other hand, too often emphasize factual content as opposed to feelings, may demonstrate a lack of interest in what the client has to say, and frequently attack or put the client in his/her place. Closed questions can often be answered in a few words or with a yes or no. However, they can still be useful at times.

Questions generally should be designed to help the client explore issues, rather than to merely provide information for the interviewer. If you rely on closed questions to structure the interview, you will find yourself forced to concentrate so hard on thinking up the next question that you may fail to listen to and attend to the client.

Open invitations to talk are extremely useful in a number of different situations. The following are some examples:

1. They help begin an interview. (Could you tell me what you'd like to talk about today? How have things been since the last time we talked together?)

2. They help get the interviewee to elaborate on a point. (Could you tell me more about that? How did you feel when that happened?)

3. They help elicit examples of specific behavior so that the helper is better able to understand what the client is describing. (Will you give me a specific example? What do you do when you get "depressed?" How do you behave? What do you mean when you say your father is hard to get along with?)

4. They help focus the client's attention on feelings. (What are you feeling as you're telling me this? How did you feel then?)

5. Questions may help you find client thinking patterns which are not immediately obvious. (What were you thinking when you said that to your boss? What thoughts were in your mind while you did that? What were you saying to yourself when the boss spoke to you and you stayed silent?)

Go through the examples above again, change them to closed questions. This exercise will help you note distinctions and differences between open and closed questions.

VARYING QUESTIONING CAN HELP CLIENTS EXPLORE ISSUES

During your next practice session, it will help if you explore various types of questions. Try asking a variety of open and closed questions. We would especially like you to try questions beginning with "how," "what," and "could" which most in the field believe give more room for helpee exploration than "why." For example, consider the different possibilities if you are asking a helpee about his or her job:

Could you tell me about how things are going on the job?[1]

---

[1] You may note that questions beginning with "could" might be interpreted as closed. A client may respond to this question with a simple "no" and say nothing more to this question. However, in North American culture, the "could" question tends to function most often as an open invitation to talk. "Could" questions have the special advantage of giving the control even more to the client as the word "could" implies that the client can decide whether or not to respond at all.

What are some of the things that trouble you about your work?

How do you feel about your boss?

Why don't you like your job?

Or consider a marital counseling session:

"Could you share an example of a typical argument?"

"What did you do when he struck you?"

"How did you feel when she cried?"

"Why do the two of you think this pattern continues?"

Could questions tend to be maximally open and pass on control to the client ("Could you tell me more?" "Could you give me an example?"). Research reveals that *could* questions put focus on the client in a comfortable way and seem to establish trust. Technically, *could* questions can be answered with a "yes" or "no" but relatively few clients stop there. *Could* questions seem to empower the client to answer questions as he or she wishes.

What questions often lead the helpee to talk about facts and specifics about a situation. *How* questions most often lead to helpee talk about process and sequence or emotions ("How did that happen?" "How do you feel about that?"). You will find varying questioning style helps clients express themselves.

Why questions typically ask clients to search for reasons undergirding their behavior, thoughts, or emotions. *Why* questions and their search for reasons often, but not always, seem to put people on the spot. They are sometimes difficult to answer for we don't always know why we or others do things. *What, how,* and *could* questions provide more room; and providing space for growth is one basic dimension of being an effective helper.

You will find that clients hesitate longer if you ask them "why." Researchers suggest that "why" leads to an internal search. At the same time, you will find many effective helpers using *why* questions. Many clients gain benefit from understanding the reasons underlying their actions. You again will have to make your own personal decisions whether or not you chose to use *why* questions.

A balance of open and closed questions is suggested in the early phases of an interview. Further, the open question "could" often provides the best overview of the situation. Later in the interview, you will often find helpees talking in relatively vague terms about a problem ("I don't get along with my lover/boss/ etc."). An open question seeking specifics ("Could you give me a specific example?") often proves to be extremely effective in defining the problem more clearly.

LESS VERBAL CLIENTS AND OPEN AND CLOSED QUESTIONS

Generally, open questions are much preferred to closed questions in the interview. Yet, it must be recognized that open questions require a verbal client, willing to share information, thoughts, and feelings with you. Following are some suggestions which may facilitate clients talking more freely with you.

Build trust at the client's pace. A central issue with hesitant clients is trust. If the client is required to meet with you or is culturally different from you, he or she may be less willing to talk. At this time, your own natural openness and social skills are particularly important. Trust building and rapport need to come first. With some clients, trust building may take a full session or more. Extensive questioning too early can make slow trust building with some clients.

Accept some randomness. Your less verbal client is not likely to give you a clear linear story of the problem. If he or she lacks trust or is highly emotionally involved in the concern, it may take some time for you to get an accurate understanding.. You may need to use a careful balance of closed and open questions to draw out the story and get "bits and pieces" before you can put a coherent story together. Regardless of what you do, keep your language as simple, straightforward, and concrete as possible.

Search for concrete specifics. Counselors and therapists talk about the "abstraction ladder." If you or the client moves "too high" on the abstraction ladder, things won't make sense to anyone. This is especially so with less verbal or emotionally distraught clients. Constantly seek to find concrete examples and stories. Avoid searching for general themes and patterns. The open question, "Could you give me a *concrete, specific* example?" is a particularly effective general concrete question. Abstractions and repeating patterns of behavior, while important, should wait until the basic facts, feelings, and thoughts have been discovered.

Seek short, concrete answers. After some trust is generated, you might begin by saying, "The teacher said you and she had an argument." Then trying asking the concrete open question, "What did your teacher say (or do)?" If you focus on concrete events and avoid evaluation and opinion in a nonjudgmental fashion, your chances for helping the client talk will be greatly expanded. You'd like to know what happened specifically, what each person said and did, and perhaps the accompanying emotions. Example concrete questions focusing on narrow specifics include:

What happened first? What happened next? What was the result? (This helps you draw out the linear sequence of the story.)

What did the other person say? What did he/she do? What did you say/do? (Focuses on observable concrete actions.)

What happened after? What did you do after? What did he/she do after? (Sometimes clients are so focused on the event that they don't yet realize it is over. This helps them see results of events.

What did you feel/think just before it happened? During? After? What do you think the other person felt? (This helps focus emotions.)

Note that each of the questions above requires relatively short answers. These are open questions which are more focused in orientation and can be balanced with some closed questions. Do not expect your less verbal client to give you full answers to these questions. You may need to ask closed questions to fill out detail and obtain specific information. ("Did he say anything?" "Where was she?" "Is your family angry?" "Did they say 'yes' or 'no'?")

The *leading* closed question is dangerous. In the examples above, you can see that a long series of closed questions can bring out the story, but it may be the client's limited responses to *your* questions rather than what the client really thought or felt.

Working with children. Children, in particular, may require considerable help from you before they are willing to share at all. With children, it really helps if you are naturally a warm, talkative person who *likes and accepts* children. Thus, it helps to begin sessions with children sharing something fun and interesting. Games, clay, and other toys in the counseling room are useful when dealing with children. You will find that children generally like to do something with their hands while they talk to you—drawing a picture during your conversation often is useful to them and to you. And, the drawings are often revealing as to what is going on in the child's life.

Summary. Undergirding the above suggestions is the reminder that your ultimate goal is to draw out 1) the general picture of what happened; 2) key facts of the situation; 3) emotions; and 4) where appropriate, draw out the reasons for the situation via the *why* question. *But do not expect this information to come in sequential order as above.*[2] If you have patience and use attending skills well, you will eventually be able to bring out their full story.

PRACTICE IN RECOGNIZING OPEN AND CLOSED QUESTIONS

The example interview below illustrates the varying types of questions. As you read the segment, classify each question as open or closed. Also circle the key words which indicate the type of question (for example, "Do," "Is," "What," "Why"). The following is a segment of an interview. Rapport and trust have already been established. The segment here starts with a summary of what the client has said previously. (Classification of Responses may be found at the end of this chapter.)

1. Helper :   Marion, so you say your are a single parent, that it has been hard for you at times, and that you would like to explore some issues about some difficulties with your children.

2. Helpee: Yes, that's right, Bill. I've been a single parent for six years now.

---

[2] Clarifying skills (minimal encourages and paraphrases), reflection of feeling, and summarization are skills of later chapters which can be used to help you and the client organize the story more fully.

___3. Helper : Could you tell me a little bit about that experience? Maybe some frustrations that you may have had as a single parent?

4. Helpee: Oh, yes, there's been many. You'd think after six years, I'd really have it all together. You know, I have a career, I'm a counselor. And I have two daughters, and a house and all the usual things, and it's really hard balancing, trying to do everything, trying to be everything for my daughters, you know, helping them with homework, disciplining them, doing everything I was supposed to do. It's just difficult managing it all.

___5. Helper : Marion, I can sense it's a big task. Could you give me a specific example of one of the issues? (Comment: Using the client's name helps personalize the interview. Do try to use the client's name periodically throughout any session.)

6. Helpee: Well, I guess the thing that's bothering me most is that I am a counselor and I work with students and then I come home at the end of the day, and I see my own kids having such a difficult time getting along. They fight with each other, they hit each other, they argue about everything, about clothes, about their friends, about the telephone, everything imaginable. And I just can't seem to be able to help them out and it's very frustrating.

___7. Helper : Could you tell me about a specific situation where you had those difficulties? (Comment: Note that the helper has used three "could" questions in a row. The client is encouraged in each one to become more specific and clear.)

8. Helpee: Well, most recently we were invited out for a lovely brunch. Some friends of ours invited us out, and the girls sat next to each other at the table and, you know, instead of using good manners like you'd think two girls could use, they started pinching and poking and hitting and teasing right at the table, and I was thoroughly embarrassed. Just so embarrassed that I couldn't stand it.

___9. Helper : Their behavior catches you by surprise. How old are the girls? (Closed question useful for context—note that "how," and "what" questions can sometimes really be closed—"What age are they?")

10. Helpee: Well, they're eleven and thirteen. You'd think by that age they'd be able to handle themselves in public.

___11. Helper : Do they hit each other all the time, Marion?

12. Helpee: Well, every day I'm sure. Quite frequently, yes.

___13. Helper : Do you hit them? (Comment: Ultimately, this is an important question to ask. Children who express violence often come from a violent home. More useful questions here might have been "How do you react when they hit each other?" or "How do you feel about hitting as a way of discipline?")

14. Helpee: No, I don't hit them and that's why I can't understand why they hit each other.

___15. Helper: Maybe they . . . Do you think they get it from their friends? Do their friends hit each other? (Comment: Here the helper has become trapped by closed questions. Closed questions can lead you to guessing what is in the client's mind and most of us aren't good "mind-readers."

16. Helpee: I don't know. I'm confused.

___17. Helper: Let's go back, Marion. Earlier you said you were embarrassed by their behavior. Could you tell me more about that? (Comment: When things aren't going well in the interview, use a basic rule of attending behavior—go back to an earlier comment and ask an open question about that issue. Again, using the client's name respectfully is a useful adjunct to rapport and sometimes can get you through your errors. *It is not the mistakes we make that are so bad—all of us will make errors. What is important is our recovery skills!*)

18. Helpee: Yes, I was embarrassed. I know that the way one's children behaves often reflects on what's going on at home. I worry about the interpretation that others are going to place on me. I don't hit my children, but I worry that others will think I do.

____ 19. Helper: Why do you think the children are hitting each other? (Comment: The potentially dangerous "why" question has been asked. It can put clients off, but if the relationship is good, sometimes useful information appears.)

20. Helpee: (breaks into tears and stammers) I think they are still reacting to the divorce. I do my best, but I can't manage them. My ex-husband used to hit us all.

In the example above you see a variety of questions used to bring out information from the client. Closed questions bring out specifics and open questions help clients explore more from their frame of reference. In this example, the helper got too involved in specifics at one point, but was able to salvage the situation. The helper did this through saying at 17. "Let's go back" and there he asked an open question about a previous topic. This is an example of how attending behavior (return to an earlier topic when you feel lost) helps you get started again.

As you gather data through open and closed questions, you can gradually learn the client's story and the client plan for the future. Again, with less verbal clients, pay special attention to focused questions which require shorter answers.

OPEN INVITATION TO TALK WITH FAMILIES AND GROUPS

Most family counselors and family therapists use questions extensively. The fast-moving and complex pace of the family session requires action on the part of the helper. Family sessions can easily swing totally out of control and the skilled use of questions provide you with powerful alternatives for action.

All of the questioning principles described in this chapter can be applied to family and group work. However, it is important to add the critical words "family" and "group" to at least some of your questions.

"How are things going with the Jones' *family*?"

"What's happening in the *family/group* right now?"

"Could you tell me something good about this *family/group*?"

"Why do you think this *group/family* is having this difficulty?"

In each of the examples above, the focus on the family or group helps each member to be aware that they are just that—a *member* of a group. Families and groups each have their own typical interaction style, rules, and norms which need to be examined.

PRACTICING OPEN INVITATION TO TALK

Again, it is your ability to use questions in your own helping interviews that is most critical. Here are specific suggestions for the practice session. You may want to refer to the earlier discussion of practice for attending behavior for more specifics.

1. *Develop a working group* of a pair, a triad, or four people.

2. *Assign roles for the practice session.*

   a. Helper

   b. Helpee

   c. Observer/operator

   d. Second observer

3. *Determine topic for role-play.* The suggested topic for this role-play is a *significant life event* such as divorce, marriage, death, obtaining a new job, an important dating experience, reactions to a new child, a significant success experience.

   The task of the helper is to use open questions to bring out the facts, feelings, reasons, and the general experience via *what, how, why,* and *could* questions. A few closed questions should be used for variety. In addition, the helper should ask at least one question aimed toward specifics. "Could you give me a specific example?"

4.   *Record interview and provide feedback.* Be specific and nonjudgmental.

5.   *Rotate roles* so all participate.

GROUP/FAMILY PRACTICE IN OPEN INVITATION TO TALK

It is suggested that couple counseling be tried for this practice session.

1.   *Develop a working group.*

   a.   Two members become the couple

   b.   Helper

   c.   Observer/recorder

2.   *Determine topic for role-play.* Any type of couple conflict is appropriate for this practice session.

3.   *Planning.* The helper's task is to draw out the couple's conflict with as much information as possible. Ideally, the helper will want to know the facts of the situation as seen by each member of the couple, the feelings each has, and any reasons the couple can generate to explain what is occurring. The task is to draw out data and information, not to problem-solve.

   During planning time, the role-played couple can generate a tentative "script" concerning their "difficulties." The observer can study the observer form and prepare any recording equipment.

4.   *Watch time carefully and provide feedback.* The role-play should last approximately 10-15 minutes. Allow 15-20 minutes for feedback.

5.   *Rotate roles as time permits.*

OPEN INVITATION FEEDBACK SHEET

1. During each practice session, count the number of open and closed questions. As you make your counts, notice the response of the helpee to the different types of questions. How long does the individual talk? What body movements do you note in response to questions?

	No. of Closed Questions	No. of Open Questions
First Videotape/Typescript		
Second Videotape/Typescript		

2. Was the helper able to use all four basic open questions? What was the result of each? Was a specific example asked for? What happened as a result?

Could: _____

What: _____

How: _____

Why: _____

Could you give me a specific example?:

_____

3. Nonverbal observations of the behavior of both helper and helpee.

_____

_____

_____

4. One specific suggestion for the helper to follow-up on would be:

_____

_____

_____

DO-USE-TEACH CONTRACT

The **Do** portion of the contract is concerned with whether or not you actually can engage in a skill. Can you demonstrate attending behavior and questioning skills in an interview? The feedback sheets are concerned with your ability to engage in or *do* the skills.

The **Use** aspect of the contract is concerned with taking the concepts of the chapter out and *using* attending behavior, questions, and other skills in your daily life. What are some of the ways you can take the concepts of questioning out and *use* them to help you in your own daily communication? Generally speaking, the most effective *use* contract is to make an agreement with yourself or with your group to practice the learning of this chapter outside of the practice workshop and then report back what happened. This practice is what will make you an expert with the skill. Report below your own unique plan to use the skill of questioning and how well it worked for you.

I plan to *use* open invitation to talk in the following context:_____

_____

_____

The result of my plan was: _____

_____

The skills of this book are designed to be shared widely. Managers in business concerns, nurses and physicians, and other professionals use these same skills in much the same fashion as counselors and helpers. The context and content may vary, but the communication skills remain the same. Similarly, parents, children, teenagers, and others use these skills. They can profit from learning what you have learned. Thus teaching the skills of this book is an important aspect of your own training and the work of the effective helper.

The **Teach** aspects of *Basic Attending Skills* is critical. You will want to turn to the teaching methodology in Chapter 8 for more data and learn how to share what you know with others. The model of teaching communication skills suggested in this book is simple, but has been proven and tested through over 25 years of clinical training with hundreds of thousands of learners in fields as varying as counseling and law, medicine and community hot-line work, and the teaching of skills to parents and elementary children.

Also, recall that teaching attending behavior and questioning skills to clients may be a particularly effective treatment mode in its own right. It provides clients with useful social skills which they can use with their families, in their work, and in many other places.

The teaching model has been described in Chapter 1. To review:

1.   *Introduction/Warm-up.* When you teach the skill, provide a brief commentary or experiential exercise on what you are going to teach.

2. *Reading about the skill.* Have the person you want to teach read information in the microcounseling manuals (particularly the summary of the skill in each chapter).

3. *Modeling.* You may want to demonstrate the skill yourself. You may want to develop your own audio or video training examples. It is most helpful to your trainee to see the skill in action.

4. *Practice.* You'll then want to have the individual you are teaching practice the skill so that real mastery can be developed. You can serve as helpee and your student can be helper.

5. *Generalization.* With your student, work on a way that they can use the Do-Use-Teach contract format.

Develop your own plans for teaching someone else the skill and summarize what happened in your own words in the space provided below or on a separate page:

Plan: _____

_____

_____

_____

Result: _____

_____

_____

_____

3. Open 5. Open 7. Open 9. Closed 11. Closed 13. Closed 15. Closed 17. Open 19. Open

Nothing is more satisfying than being heard.

The minimal encourage helps you draw out the client's story.

The paraphrase indicates that you have indeed heard client issues accurately.

CHAPTER 4

CLARIFYING: THE MINIMAL ENCOURAGE AND PARAPHRASE

The skills of attending and questioning are useful in assisting the helpee to start talking. The skills of this chapter, the minimal encourage and the paraphrase, facilitate further conversation in more depth. These skills show the helpee that you have *heard* what has been said.

You will find that the minimal encourage is a most simple skill—yet, it is one of the most powerful. The minimal encourage and the paraphrase both focus on using the key words of the client and then saying back to them the most important things they have said to you. At first glance, "saying back" what has been said sounds easy. However, accurate paraphrasing is one of the most difficult and important skills you can master.

The exercises and readings in this chapter seek to help you:

1. Recall how you have felt when you have been heard and contrast that to when you were not heard. The two skills in this chapter are critical in helping clients to feel that you have listened to their stories.

2. Define the minimal encourage and paraphrase.

3. Distinguish how the paraphrase differs from the interpretation.

4. Demonstrate the two skills in a practice interview. In addition, you may wish to try the skills in a group or family situation.

5. Use the two skills in interviews and in your daily interactions with others. You will also be asked to consider yourself as a teacher of this skill both to clients and to other helpers.

EXERCISE: WHAT DOES IT FEEL LIKE TO BE HEARD? NOT HEARD?

All of us have had times when someone didn't hear us. Perhaps you felt lost and lonely when someone didn't listen to a real concern or maybe an important accomplishment was ignored. You have also experienced the joy of someone hearing you. It is a wonderful gift when someone truly listens to you. Take a moment and think of the importance of those times. The specifics of the event need not be written, but write below the feelings that occurred in each.

I felt heard:_____

_____

_____

I wasn't heard: _____

_____

_____

With those feelings and thoughts in mind, we can examine the central skills of active listening—the minimal encourage and paraphrase. The minimal encourage and paraphrase are closely related. The first helps the client explore issues in more depth, the second facilitates accuracy of understanding and truly indicates to the other person that you have listened. Together these skills bring clarity to the counseling session.

THE MINIMAL ENCOURAGE: BASIC SKILL #3

Minimal encourages are small indicators to another person that you are with her or him. Once you have asked a question (or used any other counseling skill), you want to encourage the helpee to keep talking. You'll be surprised how very little in the way of specific counseling leads are necessary if you just encourage the helpee to "keep going."

Nonverbal minimal encourages should be considered first. They are elaborations of attending behavior. For example, your client will talk more easily if you maintain culturally appropriate eye contact, your body leans forward with interest, and you use facilitative open gestures. Head nods are used by many counselors unconsciously and seem to facilitate talk.

In short, don't be wooden; find your own natural body style of encouraging others to share themselves with you. On the other hand, beware of awkwardness and moving too much. You'd like your body to be in tune with your client.

Verbal minimal encourages are brief utterances through which you can help the client move further or into more depth. Here are some useful examples:

1. "Oh?" "So?" "Then?" "And?"

2. "Umm-hummm." "Uh-huh."

3. "Tell me more."

4. The repetition of one or two key words.

5. Simple restatement of the exact same words of the helpee's last statement.

Silence as a minimal encourage. On occasion, the most valuable minimal encourage may be silence. Professional counselors talk about "response latency time" which means the number of seconds a helper waits before making a response. Many times the helper should give the helpee *time* to respond or to continue. The most classic example of inability to develop a satisfactory waiting period before continuing is the lecturer who finishes a point and then asks the group, "Any questions?" Before anyone has a chance to respond, the lecture continues.

The importance of restating key words. When single words or short phrases are repeated back to the helpee, they almost inevitably will respond by elaborating on the concept in more detail. One of the best ways, and least intrusive, to obtain further information and opinions from a helpee is to repeat back a key word or two or the exact same words of a short phrase. Research shows that this type of minimal encouragement is used more and more by effective professionals and non-professionals.

Paraphrasing is closely related to the key word minimal encourage, but it focuses on what has been said and covers a longer time frame. In the paraphrase, you again want to use the client's key words as you say back to them the essence of their comments.

THE PARAPHRASE: BASIC SKILL #4

One of your most basic tasks is to *hear* the helpees clearly and to *let them know that they have been heard.* Accurately hearing and sensing another person is the basis for all the skills in this series. Paraphrasing is a special type of attending which demands that you demonstrate your ability accurately to "give back" to that person what he or she has said. Effective paraphrasing often implies a giving of self to another person to help them gain increased clarity.

Consider the following client statement:

> I've been having a terrible time with Joan. She just got promoted and seems to have the big head. She keeps telling me what to do. In fact, yesterday she said I wasn't doing a good job and that, if I didn't improve, she'd fire me.
>
> Minimal encourage: "Fire you?" (or "Terrible time?" or "Telling you what to do?")
>
> Paraphrase: "Bob, you're saying that the new supervisor is giving you a *terrible time* and you're concerned she may *fire you.*"

Note that the minimal encourage tends to lead Bob to elaborate in more detail on the event. And, each type of minimal encourage might lead Bob in a very different direction. By way of contrast, the paraphrase feeds back to Bob what he has been saying and indicates to Bob that he has indeed been heard. Note that some of the most important words which Bob used were repeated in identical form in the paraphrase, but that the interviewer/helper has shortened the statement picking up the essence of what has been said.

The structure of the paraphrase should be considered. The most effective paraphrases consist of:

1. The client's name and/or the pronoun "you." There is clear evidence that personalizing the paraphrase makes it more effective.

2. The most important key words of the helpee.

3. A distilled, shortened, and clarified helper statement which catches the essence of what has been said.

The Check-Out: Occasionally, check-out the accuracy of your paraphrases with the check-out, a closed question which gives the client a chance to react to your statement. Example check-out questions to follow your paraphrase are:

> Is that right? Am I close? Is that what you said?
> Am I hearing you accurately? OK?

If your paraphrase is successful, the helpee will likely reward you with words such as "exactly," "yes," or "right." If the client needs to talk in more depth, the paraphrase facilitates more extensive talk. If the client has talked enough on a topic, the paraphrase facilitates movement to a new subject. There are clients who say the same thing over and over again. Paraphrasing can help them move on to other issues.

DISTINGUISHING PARAPHRASING FROM INTERPRETATION

In encouraging and paraphrasing we seek to help the client tell his or her story with minimal influence on our part. You want to hear how the client views a conflict, experienced a trauma, or thinks about a vocational decision. In listening, give the client prime attention and focus on their view of what happened.

Consider the following interviewing situation. Note that the three helping leads— minimal encourage, paraphrase, and interpretation represent points on a continuum. The first two focus on the client's view of the situation, the interpretation on the interviewer's view of the same situation.

> Helpee: I'm really feeling lost. My Dad drinks a lot and sometimes he beats my Mom. Its really tough at home. I find it really difficult to study or even do anything.

Helper: (Minimal Encourage) "You feel lost." or "Difficult to do anything."

(Paraphrase) "You're feeling *lost* because its *really tough at home* and you can't *do anything.*" (Italics emphasize client's key words.)

(Interpretation) Sounds like your Dad is an alcoholic. That really makes it tough for any teenager.

Note that the interpretation may indeed be accurate, but it is the helper's viewpoint and may not be the client's. Helping theory holds that it is best if the client can come to the interpretation on his or her own. If you have worked with alcohol problems, you are well aware that naming a "drinking problem" as alcoholism is a big step. Thus, it is recommended that you first focus on the client's worldview through careful listening and save your interpretation until later.

Keep the following maxim in mind:

If you listen first,
client's are much more likely to accept your ideas,
advice, and interpretations later.

Even better, if you listen first,
many clients will come to useful
and correct interpretations on their own.

The above brief example should illustrate that defining the distinction between encouraging, paraphrasing, and interpretation is not an easy matter. Clearly, in each case above, the helper has *selectively attended* to what the helpee has said about the problem. The minimal encourage involves the helper minimally in what the client talks about while the paraphrase is the helper's effort to give back the essence (as the helper sees it) of what has just been said. The interpretation focuses on the helper's frame of reference rather than the client's view.

Paraphrases serve three purposes at this stage: 1) they convey to the helpee that you are with her/him, that you are trying to understand what is being said; 2) they crystallize a helpee's comment by making it more concise thus helping give better direction to the interview; and 3) they provide a check on the accuracy of the perceptions of the interviewer.

INTEGRATING QUESTIONS, ENCOURAGES, AND PARAPHRASING

Basic Attending Skills are sequenced so that you can integrate the skills as each new dimension is added. For example, when you use the skill of questioning, you still need to continue culturally appropriate attending behavior. When you add encouraging and paraphrasing, questions can be integrated to facilitate client expression.

As client's tell their stories and talk about important life events, they develop new understandings which enable them to move on and sometimes even to rewrite their past history. Your task as a listener is to draw out the client's story as accurately as you can. It is the client's story. You want to keep your ideas and reactions out of their story.

Negative example. The first example below illustrates how your own interpretations can interfere with the client's story. As you read the counselor leads, classify each one as an open or closed question (O?, C?), minimal encourage (E), paraphrase (P), or interpretation (I). Also look for check-outs (C-O) which appear very similar to closed questions, but are clearly used for a different purpose. More than one counselor lead occurs in some of the statements. (See the end of this chapter for classifications of skills.)

____ 1. Counselor: (To depressed client) What's going on with your family?

2. Client: They don't visit me at all any more.

____ 3. Counselor: They don't visit you.

____ Why do you think that is?

4. Client: They don't like me, I guess.

___5. Counselor: Perhaps, it's because you don't pay any attention to them.

  6. Client: (defensively) Well, they don't pay any attention to me either.

As is common with many depressed clients, this client gives relatively short responses. There is a need to focus on specifics and encourage more concrete description.

Positive example.

___7. Counselor: You say that *they don't pay attention to you.*

___ Could you tell me how it went the last time they came to see you?
(Note the focus on concrete, specific events. This is useful with all clients, but particularly with less verbal clients.)

  8. Client: It wasn't good.
(Note that helper open questions don't always get long answers. With such clients, move to the search for concrete specifics.)

___9. Counselor: *It wasn't good.*

___ Could you give me a specific example of something that *wasn't good?*
(It is important to use client key words in questions. This helps clients explore issues of underlying meaning in more depth.)

  10. Client: Well, last time Mom didn't like the way I was wearing my hair. She had hardly got here, but she was trying to get me to fix it like she wants it.

___11. Counselor: Your Mom wanted you to wear your hair the way *she wants it.*
(Note use of client key words.)

12. Client: Yeah, she's always telling me what to do. It's almost easier to have nothing to do with her.

____ 13. Counselor: Sue, I hear you saying that your Mom wanted you to do things her way; and it's easier for you to have *nothing to do with her.*

____   Is that right?

14. Client: Exactly. I just clam up, and I don't say anything.

____ 15. Counselor: Uh-huh, *You clam up.*

____   Tell me more about what happens.

16. Client: I used to fight back when my Mom picked at me. Somehow I learned it is easier to just sit and do nothing and ignore her.

____ 17. Counselor: So, Susie, I hear you saying you don't pay your parents much attention because you've found that it is *easier to sit back and do nothing.*

In the first example above, you have seen that clients can be "turned off" by your interpretations of their situations. The second example focuses on the client's interpretation of the visit. Through questioning, minimal encourages, and paraphrasing, the client's version of the story is brought out. Recall the following maxim:

The first step in helping a client change the meaning of stories or their behavior, feelings, or thoughts is to hear their story as they interpret it.

Finally, note in the above example how the counselor used the major, key words of the client whether using the minimal encourage or the paraphrase. Furthermore, questions which include key words of the client are also preferred.

USING THE CLARIFYING SKILLS WITH GROUPS AND FAMILIES

The minimal encourage and paraphrase are used with equal effectiveness with groups and in family work. You can help bring out less verbal group or family members through focused and concrete open questions coupled with encouraging and paraphrasing. In such cases, the skills are used in much the same fashion as with individual work.

More difficult, but equally important, is using the paraphrase with the group or family as a whole. Here you need to use the key words "family" and "group" and paraphrase the essence of what all are saying. For example:

Mother: Sonia isn't eating. We're afraid she's bulemic.

Father: No, Mother, I don't think she is. She just wants to keep her weight down.

Counselor: Sonia? (Minimal encourage)

Daughter: I don't have any problem. Like Dad says, Mom's just making a fuss.

Counselor: The *family* seems to look at Sonia differently. Mom's worried about bulemia, but Dad thinks she's just trying to keep her weight down. Sonia thinks that Mom's just making a fuss. How do such differences of opinion get worked out in this *family?*

The example is obviously shortened. If you are working with an individual (and it could be Dad, Mom, or daughter), you would focus on how one person thinks. In family therapy and groupwork, you have several individuals to respond to; but you also need to be aware of focusing on the group or family as a whole.

When paraphrasing what is happening in a group or family, you do much the same as you would with an individual; but you focus your helping statements on the group as a whole. A common family therapy and group technique is to ask each member of the group the same question and then to talk about how the family or group works on the question together.[1]

PRACTICING THE MINIMAL ENCOURAGE AND THE PARAPHRASE

1. *Develop a working group.*

2. *Assign roles* as helper, helpee, operator/observer, and second observer.

3. *Determine topic for role-play.* While any topic may be used, we have found talking about a family story is most useful. This can be the family of origin or the present living family of the client. The family story can be positive or negative, past or present. The task of the helper is to use attending behavior and questions to bring out the story and then to use a variety of minimal encourages to keep the helpee talking and elaborating. At several points in the interview, the helper should paraphrase what the helpee has been saying using the key words of the client.

4. *Watch time carefully and provide feedback.*

5. *Rotate roles.*

GROUP/FAMILY PRACTICE IN MINIMAL ENCOURAGES AND PARAPHRASING

It is suggested that structured group counseling be tried for this practice session. However, couple counseling or family counseling may be practiced as well, if you prefer.

1. *Develop specific roles for the practice session.*

   a. Three or more individuals form the "group".

   b. Group facilitator.

---

[1] Another useful technique is circular questioning. Here you ask one member of the group how she or he thinks another member would answer the question. Through using this type of questioning, you will often discover unsaid things in the group or family.

c. Observer/recorder.

2. *Determine topic for role-play.* Three possible topics for the group are: a) a current problem in ethnic or race relations in the community; b) problems which members might have in their work setting; c) future career plans of the group members.

3. *Planning.* The helper's task is complex in group work such as this. First, recall that your goal is to draw out individual and group stories, not problem resolution. Thus, you would like to:

    a) Draw out each individual's story using questioning, minimal encourages, and paraphrasing.

    b) Find group themes. You will find that some members of the group tell similar stories and you can relate them together through paraphrasing. Furthermore, the group itself will have a style and you can use the key word *group* to help members look at the group interaction.

    c) Focus on the topic itself. Not only do individuals and groups have stories, but you will find it possible to construct a joint picture of the problem or topic as the several individuals view it.

        Groupwork makes it possible for (a) individuals to tell their stories; (b) see how their stories are similar to and different from others; and (c) learn more about the problem or topic.

4. *Watch time carefully and provide feedback.* A meaningful group interaction will take at least 30 minutes, and the same amount of time will be required for feedback and exploration of what happened. In the feedback session, give special attention to the role of the group facilitator.

RATING AND BEHAVIORAL COUNT SHEET FOR PARAPHRASING AND MINIMAL ENCOURAGES[2]

List the main words of each helper statement and indicate whether it is an open or closed question, minimal encourage, paraphrase, or other skill (O?, C?, ME, P, O). You will find that listing the main words of each helper statement will enable you to reconstruct the total session after it is completed even if you do not video or audiorecord.

With group or family practice, observers may also need to make brief notes of group and family members' comments.

____ 1. _____

____ 2. _____

____ 3. _____

____ 4. _____

____ 5. _____

____ 6. _____

____ 7. _____

____ 8. _____

____ 9. _____

____ 10. _____

[2] Continue this format on a separate sheet of paper. You will find that maintaining records of individual, group, or family interviews will greatly facilitate your feedback sessions and your understanding of what happened. Use this feedback sheet as you practice other skills in this book as well.

DO-USE-TEACH CONTRACT

How are you going to use and teach these concepts?

Do I learned or noticed in practicing and/or observing these skills

_____

_____

_____

_____

Use I plan to use this skill outside this practice session as follows:

_____

_____

_____

_____

Teach I plan to teach this skill to others as follows:

_____

_____

_____

_____

---

1. O? 3. E, O? 5. Int. 7. P , O? 9.E, O? 11. P 13. P, C-O 15. E, E 17. P

The artistic counselor catches the feelings and emotions of the client

Our emotional side often guides our thoughts and actions, even without our conscious awareness.

CHAPTER 5

RESPONDING TO FEELINGS AND EMOTIONS

Empathy has been defined as accurately hearing and understanding the client. Basic to empathy are the several attending skills of this book. However, many believe that the skill of reflection of feeling—the accurate sensing of the emotional world of the helpee—is the most important skill for developing empathic understanding.

The exercises and readings in this chapter seek to help you:

1. Name emotions and understand their importance in the helping interview.

2. Define the skill of reflection of feeling and offer some practice in distinguishing it from other skills.

3. Examine some gender and multicultural issues around emotion. The skill of acknowledging feelings may be helpful in reflecting emotion to many clients.

4. Demonstrate the skill of reflection of feeling in a practice individual interview. In addition, you may wish to try the skill in family and group practice sessions.

5. Use reflection of feelings in your own interview practice and in daily life. You will also be encouraged to think about teaching this skill to others.

NAMING FEELINGS AND EMOTIONS

While many of us like to think we make decisions rationally, in truth we aren't really satisfied unless the decision "feels good." Similarly, we may talk about our problems in an intellectual fashion; but, unless we deal with the emotions underlying the issue, we are likely to continue old, ineffective behavior.

For example, you may work with the child of an alcoholic family or with someone who experienced abuse. The facts of the situation may be clear, but the emotions may be buried. In cases such as this, your main task may be to uncover and help the client deal with complex, sometimes troubling and confusing emotions. Knowing that one should leave a bad relationship is one thing—having the emotional strength to do it is another.

Emotions are important in all helping relationships. The client may rationally choose a vocation, but later feel unsatisfied because emotional issues were ignored. The facts and the reasons for their decision may be clear; but, until the client deals with underlying feelings about the job, something will remain unresolved.

Feeling words.. As a first step toward responding to a client's feelings, you must be able to recognize and name those feelings. Some basic emotional states are listed below followed by some other related words. Extend that list yourself with even more words. The richer your feeling vocabulary, the more you will be able to understand the world of the client. Start with the basic "mad, glad, sad, scared."

Mad: anger, annoyed, hate _____

Glad: joy, happy, excited_____

Sad: misery, hurt, guilt _____

Scared: shy, worried, fear_____

Additional emotional words which fit in one or more of the above categories include: *relieved, exhausted, embarrassed, inadequate, indifferent, courageous, infatuated, tender*—the list of feeling words can go on and on. List as many additional feeling words as you can either here or on a separate page.

_____

_____

_____

Mixed feelings. Often your clients will present confused or mixed emotions. In many situations, we feel combinations of several emotions. We may be in love, but anxious about the result. We may be very pleased about a new job opportunity, but scared at the same time. Sorting out these mixed feelings is an important part of the helping process.

Some key examples of mixed feelings include the words *upset, torn, mixed up, confused, unsure, perplexed, troubled, and ambivalent.* These words are not usually important underlying feelings. Rather, they often represent a surface description of complex feelings. A helpee may say that he or she is *upset* about a difficult relationship. If you listen further, you may find that the underlying feelings are *hurt, anger, rejection, love, caring,* and others.

When you hear words which represent complex, mixed feelings, reflect the surface word, but continue your questioning to find underlying, more basic dimensions of emotion. For example, "You say you feel *torn.* Could you tell me more about what that word *torn* means to you?"

Feelings expressed as metaphor. Some clients will talk about feeling like a *"limp dish rag,"* that they have *"reached the bottom of the barrel,"* or perhaps they feel like *"a case of dynamite about to explode."* In each case, single words really can't express the depth of emotion. You will also want to be aware of metaphor as an important key to understanding the emotional world of your client. Metaphors are also like mixed feelings—there is more going on than just the surface expression.

Both verbal and nonverbal clients may find it easier to express their emotions via metaphor. Ask your client to imagine the way they feel and then to describe what it is like for them. Some of the most successful therapists and counselors work very effectively through metaphoric expressions. Metaphors could be described as the poetry of emotional life.

What are some emotional metaphors that occur to you?

_____

_____

Nonverbal feelings. Be alert to the client's smile, the jiggling foot (which may indicate restlessness, anger, or boredom), and any form of body movement. Crossed arms or legs may indicate anger or defensiveness, and wiping one's nose may indicate personal discomfort. Emotions are located in the body, and careful observation of body movement will often give you better clues as to what is occurring in clients than the words they say.

Nonverbal feelings, however, are sometimes gender and culturally determined. Note body movements, eye contact breaks, etc., but always with some caution until you understand the meaning of the gesture or movement for the unique person from a unique cultural background.

Relating at the emotional level is difficult for many of us as we have been taught in many cultures to control feelings. Yet, our feelings often obscure and confuse our thought processes. This very important skill of helping requires you to work hard to achieve both sensitivity to others and mastery of the skill.

REFLECTION OF FEELING: BASIC SKILL # 5

How can you help others to express the central concerns they are experiencing? One excellent way is to listen for and respond to the feelings of the client. Through reflecting feelings, you can facilitate the client's movement toward more complete self-acceptance and self-understanding. You would like to communicate to the client that you can accurately sense the world as he or she is feeling and experiencing it.

Most central to this skill is being alert to and responding to the *feeling* being expressed rather than the *content. What* the client is saying is the *content* portion of the message. You must also listen to *how* the client gives a message. For example, the client may speak more quickly when communicating enthusiasm, more slowly when communicating discouragement, etc. It is this *feeling* portion of the communication to which you are asked to give special attention.

In reflecting feelings, the following steps are most essential:

1. The feelings must be named. This may be through the actual words used by the helpee, through metaphor, or through observation of nonverbal communication.

2. Use a sentence structure such as "You seem to feel...," "Sounds like you feel . . ." "I sense you're feeling..." and add the labeled emotion.

3. The context may be paraphrased for additional clarification: "You seem to feel _____ when _____." or "You feel _____ because _____." Here we have a combined paraphrase/reflection of feeling.

4. If you are not sure of the emotion, add a check-out "Is that close?" "Is that the way you feel?" "Is that right?" This gives the client a chance to reflect on, add to, or correct your emotional reading.

Reflections of feelings are most often useful if immediate here and now feelings in the interview are labeled and worked through. Rather than working in the past tense ("You felt _____"), try to reflect present in-the-moment feelings ("Right now, you feel _____").

Let us expand on reflection of feeling with the acknowledgment of feeling and issues related to gender and culture.

ACKNOWLEDGING FEELING: MULTICULTURAL AND GENDER CAUTIONS

Trust is important if your clients are to share their feelings with you. However, even in the most trusting relationship, some clients will have difficulty sharing and exploring their feelings with you.

For example, in White, North American and many other cultures, men are expected to hold back their feelings. You aren't a "real man" if you allow yourself to feel emotion. While many men can and do express their feelings in the helping interview, some should not be pushed too hard in this area in the first phases of counseling. Later, with trust, exploration of feelings becomes more acceptable.

In general, women in all cultures are more in touch with and more willing to share feelings than men. Nonetheless, this will vary with the cultural group. Some cultures (for example, Asian, Native American) at times pride themselves on their ability to control emotions. However, this may also be true with those of British and Irish extraction.

African-Americans and other minorities have learned over time that it may not be safe to share oneself openly with White Americans. In cross-cultural counseling situations, trust needs to be built before you can expect in-depth discussion of emotions.

The *acknowledgment of feeling,* a shortened form of the reflection of feeling, can be helpful with many men and clients who are culturally different from you. Rather than delve deeply into emotion, the helper simply notes the feelings briefly and moves on without further probing. The only real difference between a reflection of feeling and acknowledgment of feeling is that the acknowledgment occurs briefly in passing form whereas the reflection of feeling often becomes a major focus of the interview. For example:

> Sounds like that made you angry. And what happened next?

> It hurt you then. What happened just before?

In the examples above, the helper briefly acknowledges feelings and moves on.

Minorities and women may experience discrimination, racism, or sexism as part of their daily life experience. If you are a majority person or a male, trust may be more difficult to generate. Acknowledging the reality of discrimination, racism, and sexism and its personal and group hurt can be an important part of the trust-building process. Similarly, a minority person working with majority clients may expect some distrust toward them as well. The acknowledgment of feelings of possible distrust may be helpful if used carefully. For example:

> Right now, you're dubious about sharing this with me.

For a client to share his or her emotional experience with you is an expression of trust. You must earn that trust with each client.

PRACTICE EXERCISES IN REFLECTING FEELINGS

In the examples below, you will have an opportunity to select statements which indicate that you understand the client's feelings and internal emotions. Select the statement which would most likely evoke a client response of, "That's right!" Label each response as a question, paraphrase, minimal encourage, or response to feeling.

Helpee: So I'm wondering if you can help me find a new major. (pause) I suppose if I did find one, I'd just foul up again.

Helper: a. You really want to find another major, but you're not sure it would work out.

b. You feel very discouraged right now, but you still have some hope for pulling it out.

c. You'd just foul up things again.

d. What majors are you considering?

e. Why do you feel that way?

In this first example, *b* is the only reflection of feeling. Note that a positive emotion as well as the negative has been reflected. Helper lead *a* is a reasonably good paraphrase, but ignores the underlying emotional aspects of the helpee's communication. *C* is minimal encourager which may lead to more feeling discussion. Helper lead *d* is a question and tends to be a topic jump leading the helpee away from self-exploration into a new area. Finally, *e* is another question which does partially respond to feeling; but the "why" dimensions tend to put the helpee on the spot with a very difficult question to answer at this point.

Helpee: What do you think I ought to do—run away, get a divorce, or just give in and take it? I feel so sad and lost.

Helper: a. There just doesn't seem to be any way out!

b. (Noting tears) You feel *really* sad right now.

c. Are you thinking seriously of running away?

d. (Silence)

e. You're really concerned and troubled. It's really getting to you.

Example 2 has two possible reflections of feeling—*b* and *e*. Either could be appropriate. *B* is an accurate reflection and shows that the client has been heard. *After* hearing full emotional expression, the counselor can later bring in more supportive and helpful data. The temptation in moments like this is to comfort, give sympathy, and provide answers. We believe it best to allow full emotional expression before moving on. Response *a,* a paraphrase, might very well be as successful as the reflection of feeling as it seems to catch the essence of the client's state of being.

C by outward appearances would be an ineffective question, unless the context warrants it. The minimal encourager of silence might be very effective but, of course, is not a reflection of feeling. Response *e* is another reflection and may be useful. It does not seem to go into as much depth as *b* but may be more appropriate depending on the total situation. In reflecting feelings, it often helps to use the major feeling words of the client even though you might add other words as well.

Helpee: You know, it's funny, but when I talk to you, I just feel shaky. It's the silliest thing!

Helper: a. Are you anxious in many situations?

b. You wonder why you do this.

    c. Right now you feel very shaky talking to me; it confuses you to feel that way.

    d. Could you share a little more about how you feel toward me?

    e. You're laughing as you tell me you feel shaky and scared.

The final example has two reflections of feeling, *c* and *e*. *C* has the advantage of here and now immediacy, *e* the advantage of pointing out the mixed messages of feelings. Question *a* may be a good approach, *if* the feelings have already been explored and are known and acknowledged; it does respond to emotion and gives the client room to explore. It would be unwise, however, if this is new information.

Question *d* has immediacy and gives the client room to explore emotion, thus underlining the fact that one need not stick exclusively to reflections to help others express their emotions. Questions, however, still do not fully acknowledge the experience of the helpee. *B* impresses us as a poor minimal encourage, but even this response could be good *if* the counselor's vocal tone is warm and supportive. Your personhood may be more important than what you say.

The above examples illustrate an important point. *No single response is going to be "right" or "wrong."* What you want is to have several alternatives available. We obviously favor, at this point, the reflective listening skills—especially giving attention to feelings. At other times you'll find advice, interpretation, and other skills useful with your clients. It is your ability to have many possibilities in reserve which will enable you to reach many clients.

SORTING OUT COMPLEX MIXED FEELINGS

Very few of us have what we might call "pure" emotions. Stress thus far has focused primarily on identifying and reflecting single emotions.

What are mixed or ambivalent feelings? All of us experience them daily, some of them produce deep conflict and problems difficult to resolve. Here are some common situations which we all face:

An examination is coming up which is very important. Your best friend suggests a movie.

> The mixed feelings underlying this decision might include *enjoyment* of movies, *fear* of failing the exam, *boredom* with studying, *caring* for your friend, etc. Resolution of even a simple decision such as this can be facilitated by exploring the many rich and varied emotional factors.

You face a major conflict with a loved one.

> The mixed feelings here may include positive feelings of *caring, love,* and *trust.* The negative feelings *(hurt, anger, fear)* conflict with the positive. Sorting out such mixed feelings is often a basic goal of counseling.

Often complex feelings are hidden by words such as "confusion," "torn," and "ambivalent." If a client says he or she is confused, it is important to use questions and reflection to discover the more precise feelings underneath the vague term of confusion. Too often counselors and interviewers settle for the feeling of confusion and fail to find the underlying complex emotions.

How does a helper cope with the wealth of emotion underlying key decisions? The beginning is reflection of identified feelings plus focused questions which help the client explore emotional experience.

Useful skills in facilitating this exploration are:

1. Noting of double messages and mixed feelings. The body might say one thing while the words say something else. For example, "You sound like you are very sure of yourself, but your body seems to be giving a different message." This lead, of course, is best reserved for those clients who are aware of body language and its meaning. It does no good to reflect emotions which the helpee will only deny.

2. Questions which provide openings for the individual to share more emotional experiences in words. "What are your feelings?" "What's going on in your body as you say that?" "How did you feel when that happened?"

3. Reflections of feeling which name the mixed emotions.

4. Checking-out the client's reaction to your reflection. "Is that close to the way you feel?" "Does that make sense?"

More than one emotion is shown in the following examples. Name the emotions and then write how you might respond to them. Use reflections, questions, and the check-out to help clients explore their underlying emotions.

Client: Things have been going better with my husband's drinking lately, and I'm feeling more hopeful. But my friends at Alanon (support group for families of alcoholics) worry me. They say its only a phase.

What feelings do you note? _____

How would you respond? _____

_____

Client: (Having just gone through a divorce.) It's been such a struggle to become independent, and I've waited so long. I guess I didn't anticipate the feeling of rootlessness that it was going to bring.

What feelings do you note? _____

How would you respond? _____

_____

Client: Gee, I really feel confused. One side of me says, hey, let's move to that new job. It's exciting and challenging. The other side of me feels afraid. And I end up just feeling torn and confused, I'm not sure what I want.

What feelings do you note? _____

How would you respond? _____

Transcript of Reflection of Feeling

Making decisions is not always a rational process. The emotions and feelings underlying the decision often determine what the person decides. In the following brief example you will find that the rational facts of an important job decision are less impactful on the final decisions than the underlying emotions.

The following transcript is particularly effective in its use of reflection of feeling. As you classify the helping leads, you will discover extensive use of the skill. In addition, note the way that questions are often focused on exploration of feelings; and you will even find some minimal encourages which focus on feelings. In cases where reflections and paraphrases are combined, note them both in classifications. Classify leads as O?, C?, ME, P, and RF. Note the check-out with a C0. (See the end of this chapter for classification of listening skills.)

____1. Helper: Could you tell me about your new job opportunity?

2. Client: Well, Helper, it's really an exciting one. It's in another state and the colleagues are absolutely fantastic, the salary is a lot better than I have. And I certainly could use the money.

____3. Helper: You sound really excited about it.

4. Client: I really am. It's really just like I feel the opportunity of a lifetime. Really the opportunity of a lifetime. But . . . ? Even as I talk I sort of say, wow, I'm not quite sure what that would mean. A long way from here, gee, the kids are here and in college; and I'd like to be with them and that's a long way away.

___ 5. Helper: You sound sort of hesitant—anxious about it? *(The questioning tone of voice serves as a check-out. Here the helper has given the emotional word to the client.)*

6. Client: Exactly. I really do get anxious because the opportunity is fantastic; and, yet, there are a lot of things holding me here, too. For example, you know, I mentioned the kids, I've made a lot of friends. I like the people I work with, I don't have any real strong...nothing really pushing me away, it's more an exciting new challenge. And yet, the thought of leaving where I am, it does make me feel very anxious.

The next helper lead summarizes what has been said so far. You are asked to classify the three parts of the summary. The summary will be discussed in the next chapter.

___ 7. Helper: As I hear you saying, you've talked about the excitement about moving, a new challenge, the people you'll be working with and that sounds very exciting.

___ And on the other hand, you've got some nice things going here. You've got colleagues that you've worked through lots of relationships with, and you understand them. Finally, you've got your kids here.

___ And so there's kind of confusion between the two, and you know, what looks better. The excitement out there or your feelings for your family and your comfort here. Am I hearing you accurately? *(The mixed feelings around the decision are confronted.)*

8. Client: You sure are. What I'm sure of here is that I do like to go to work, I find the people I work with compatible, I find them interesting, I like the students. I certainly love New England, and that's

certainly a major plus. It's fall now; and it really feels pretty good, really nice. At the same time, New England has certain problems. The economy is ghastly. I get very frustrated and angry with the fact that there's never enough time and money to do what I want to do.

___9. Helper: Frustrated and angry about...?

10. Client: Well, for example, frustrated and angry in terms of, like, I find myself trying to do a good job, but worrying that the job may not exist in a year or so. The economy just doesn't seem very promising.

___11. Helper: So you're wondering if this move...if now's the time to make the move?

___ What has been your experience with moving in the past? And how have you felt when you moved?

12. Client: Well, that's helpful. When I first...the first major move I made was from Pennsylvania to Colorado; and that was an absolute up. I just felt that anytime I could move, I could leave all the mistakes behind me; and you know me, I had plenty of mistakes! As I got to Colorado . . . and I just fit in, wonderful time, loved it professionally. It just was really a real high, professionally, at least.

___13. Helper: So that first move was excellent, and it was exciting, wonderful.

14. Client: Really exciting. It was really good.

___15. Helper: And then what happened?

___ 16. Client: And then I moved to New England; and, when we arrived here, nobody basically spoke to us for the first six months. New England's a great place but it takes a long time to get in.

___ 17. Helper: So you felt a little lonely when you first got here?

___ 18. Client: You really caught it! It was absolute agony. And I mean literally; even now at this moment, it almost brings tears to my eyes about leaving those people I cared so much about in Colorado. And now...and it took me, I'd say, four years before I felt comfortable here.

___ 19. Helper: So it took you a long time to settle in here; and you're maybe thinking that it might take a long time to settle in a distant, new state. Is that close to what you think and feel? *(Note that while emotions are central in this example, the facts of the situation remain important.)*

___ 20. Client: I don't only think, I know, and the thought of leaving my kids here would be very painful, because they wouldn't be coming to visit as often.

___ 21. Helper: How would that make you feel?

___ 22. Client: It's terrifying, because maybe I wouldn't be that much ahead financially. And just that whole pain of separation and then starting again with new people would be really overwhelming.

___ 23. Helper: So you're wondering if the pain is worth all the excitement of the new job, that even though there'll be an exciting new job and a new challenge, with all the pain, would it be worth it? You know, in terms of the pain. The trade-off. *(This also is a summary as it integrates much of what has been said so far.)*

24. Client: And, at this moment, as I start balancing, maybe it isn't worth it.

This transcript is presented as it illustrated clearly the importance of underlying emotions. You will find that often your clients come to you with little awareness of how important emotional experience is in their decision-making and total life process. Focusing on and reflecting feelings can be an invaluable part of the counseling and therapy process. Reflecting feelings can be helping at its best.

REFLECTION OF FEELINGS IN GROUP AND FAMILY INTERVIEWS

Family problems often rest on a sometimes explosive foundation of emotion. The problem with the family may be presented rationally and clearly; and, yet, you can sense the strong feelings underneath. The same applies to group sessions. Individuals present issues, then you find what they are *really* feeling as the group progresses.

Not only do members of families and members of groups have feelings, but there is also a joint "feeling tone" which is not the feelings of any one member, but speaks to the whole group. For example, you may work with a group who does not know each other well. The various members may be expressing themselves clearly, but underlying disagreements or emotions may be buried. Your task as a group leader or family counselor is to help the members examine deeper emotional issues in a safe fashion.

In group and family work, you will want to acknowledge and reflect individual feeling. In addition, you may also want to focus your reflections on the total group or family itself through questions oriented to emotion, minimal encourages, and reflection of feeling.

This *family/group* seems to have something unsaid right now. What do you think it is?

There seems to be tension in the air for all of us right now. What is the *group/family* feeling?

This *group/family* has been sitting here for awhile. What emotions and feelings seem to represent this *group/family?*

What was the impact of what was just said on the *group/family?*

The *group/family* seems (sad, glad, relieved, angry, etc.) right now.

Note that the skill remains the same, but the focus turns to the total group or family. As in all other listening skills discussed in this book, reflection and exploration of feelings which focus on the group as a whole can be especially valuable.

PRACTICING REFLECTION OF FEELING

1. *Develop a working group.*

2. *Assign roles* as helper, helpee, operator/observer, and second observer.

3. *Determine topic for role-play.* It is suggested that the helpee talk about a time which involved some type of separation from loved ones. Important separations in life include leaving home for work or education, one's own divorce or the divorce of one's parents, the death of a loved one, children growing up and leaving home. There are many important separations we face over the life cycle. These separations often form an important part of the issues which you will face in helping relationships.

   A note to the helpee—you must be emotionally expressive, or it will be very difficult for your helper to reflect feelings.

   Give special attention to complex, mixed emotions. If you hear vague feelings such as "confused," "torn," or other ambivalent messages, use questions to help sort out the deeper feelings underneath. You will find yourself naturally including reflection of feeling with the paraphrase.

4. *Watch time carefully and provide feedback.*

5. *Rotate roles.*

GROUP/FAMILY PRACTICE IN REFLECTION OF FEELING

It is suggested that family counseling be tried for this practice session.

1. *Develop a working group.*

    a. Three members become the family

    b. Helper

    c. Observer/recorder

2. *Determine topic for role-play.* Family problems often arise during key times of separation during the life cycle. The couple may be divorcing, moving to a new location, a child may be leaving home for college, a grandparent may be moving in, one of the parents may have lost a job, or anyone in the family may be seriously ill.

3. *Planning.* The helper's task is to draw out the family separation issue but to pay special attention to individual feelings. Ideally, the helper will want to know the interpretations and feelings around the separation situation as seen by each member of the family. The task is to draw out data and feelings, not to problem-solve at this time.

    The helper should look for a general family feeling tone. How is this family functioning, as a whole unit, at an emotional level?

    During planning time, the role-played family can generate a tentative "script" concerning their separation issue. The observer can study the observer form and prepare any recording equipment.

4. *Watch time carefully and provide feedback.* The role-play should last approximately 10-15 minutes. Allow 15-20 minutes for feedback.

5. *Rotate roles as time permits.*

RATING AND BEHAVIORAL COUNT SHEET FOR REFLECTION OF FEELING

1. During the practice session, list the emotions you observe in the helpee or family/group—both verbal and nonverbal.

    _____

    _____

2. List each reflection of feeling used by the helper. Use exact words as closely as possible. How well do they match the feelings listed in #1 above?

    _____

    _____

    _____

    _____

3. List observations of non-verbal behavior.

    _____

    _____

    _____

4. Cite one strength of the interview and one specific area on which the helper might want to improve. Be as direct and clear as possible.

    _____

    _____

5.   If a second observer is available, record each helper statement. In this way the content of the session can be readily reconstructed.

_____

_____

_____

A DO-USE-TEACH CONTRACT

1.   I did use reflection of feelings during the practice sessions (when, where, and with what effect?):

_____

_____

_____

2.   You will find it interesting and helpful to practice acknowledging feelings in your daily life—at restaurants with a busy waitperson, with clerks in the story, with busy co-workers on the job, even with family members. There are many emotions you encounter constantly.

I plan to use this new skill outside this session in the following manner:

_____

_____

_____

---

3.   At this point in the book, you may want to think about how you could help train peer counselors or family members in listening skills. Naming and reflecting feelings is an important part of any such training.

My plans to teach this important skill to someone else are as follows:

_____

_____

_____

1. O? 3. RF 3. 5. RF 7. RF, P. RF-CO, 9. E 11. P, O? 13. RF 15. O? 17 RF 19. P,RF, CO, 21. O? 23. P, RF.

To summarize, put the client's thoughts, feelings, and behaviors together accurately.

CHAPTER 6

SUMMARIZATION: INTEGRATING CLIENT BEHAVIOR, THOUGHTS, AND FEELINGS

Summarization is a rather straightforward skill. Doing it well, however, is another matter. The concept is similar to the paraphrase and reflection of feeling but requires deeper concentration on helpee statements over time. It also requires you to synthesize a number of client statements into a more integrated whole.

The exercises and readings in this chapter seek to help you:

1. Understand how the skill of summarization helps organize interviews and client thinking about problems.

2. Define the skill of summarization.

3. Demonstrate the summarization skill in a practice interview and to consider its implications for family and group interviews.

4. Use summarization in your daily practice of interviewing and to consider how you might teach this important integrative skill to others.

SUMMARIZATION AND ITS IMPORTANCE IN ORGANIZING INTERVIEWS

The clients who come to you are often confused. They may have so many things going on in their lives that they don't know which way to turn. They may experience mixed emotions. Important facts regarding decisions may be overlooked. At other times, you may work with clients who seem very organized, but actually are rigid and missing important parts of their own daily life.

One of the major tasks you face as a helper, counselor, or therapist is to help clients organize themselves, clarify thinking and feelings, and, in the process, learn how to look at themselves more clearly. When we use summarization, we attempt to recapitulate, to condense, and to organize the essence of what clients have said.

The skill of summarization involves listening to a client over a period of time (from three minutes to a complete session or more), picking out relationships among key issues, and restating them back accurately to the client.

By using summarizations periodically, we can check out our perceptions with helpees to see how accurate our listening has been. Also, this skill aids helpees in seeing their own personal distortions. By accurately condensing what has been said, we offer helpees a chance to examine their own thinking.

In the space below, you may want to brainstorm or list some examples where you have felt disorganized. This could be in your own personal life or even in your own past work as an interviewer.

_____

_____

_____

_____

SUMMARIZATION: BASIC SKILL #6

Summarization is not often identified as a skill used in counseling. We are prone to think of attending behavior, reflection of feelings, the use of questions, and paraphrasing as the essential dimensions of listening skills. Yet, it is summarization which brings together information gained via these other skills and helps the client "pull it all together."

The key purpose of summarization is to help another individual integrate behavior, thoughts, and feelings. A secondary purpose is to check on whether or not you as helper have fallen into distortion. When a summarization is accurate and without distortion, it can help move the interview from exploration to action and problem solving. A good summarization provides a crucial lever, indicating to the helpee that you have heard the entire story thus far.

Summarizations are similar to paraphrases and reflections of feeling. A summarization of feeling is close to a reflection of feeling with one major exception: a summarization of feeling covers a longer time period and involves a broad range of feelings which the helpee has expressed. A summarization of content is similar to a paraphrase but differs in the same respect. The temporal period covered by a summary is longer. A paraphrase deals with the client's last few sentences or a short paragraph. A summary puts together a number of client paragraphs, an entire session, or perhaps even issues expressed over a series of several interviews.

Usually, we do not distinguish between a summarization of feeling and a summarization of content. This is because you usually want to integrate *both* emotions and content in your interviewing practice. The distinction between summarization of content and summarization of feeling remains useful, however, as it reminds us that we need to think of both dimensions when we help clients integrate their thinking.

Examples of Summarization

The following summarizations cover both emotional and objective content:

> To a helpee who is struggling with a difficult employer and has been told of a possible layoff:

> > As I understand what you have been saying over the past hour, there seem to be three key things: 1) you're very angry and hurt at what's being done to you; 2) nonetheless, you feel that you need and want to look at what you can do to improve your job performance; and 3) as we've talked, it sounds like you would like to meet again next week to work on that. *Have I heard you accurately?*

> To a parent troubled by a son taking drugs (third session of a continuing series):

> > You now seem to be feeling very aware that your control of your son, making him "toe the line" on every issue, may have been overly harsh and one of the reasons he joined the drug scene.

This contrasts with your feelings of anger the first time we met when you said that the school was at fault. You also seem to be saying that you "gave up" on him too soon and now want to take a new, more balanced approach. *Is that right? Have I missed anything?*

In each of the examples above, the helper gives back to the helpee the essence of what has been said while exploring both cognitive and emotional dimensions of the problem. Before moving on, note that the check-out is especially important so that you can see if you have heard accurately and not distorted the message.

Specific behaviors and things to think about as you summarize:

1. Use questions, minimal encourages, paraphrases, and reflections of feeling, to indicate to the helpee that you are attending and with her/him.

2. Note important behaviors, thoughts, and feelings throughout the interview. Look for repeating patterns. Also, search for inconsistencies in feelings or facts. Most people have mixed feelings toward important people or situations, and reflecting to the helpee these mixed feelings may be especially valuable.

    At other times, you will find your client telling you two different stories in the same session. Summarization helps you and the client clarify what has happened.

3. When the helpee is making a decision, give special attention to central threads of information throughout the session. Note the main issues so you can give them back later.

4. At several points during the session, time your comments appropriately and summarize for the helpee what you have heard so far.

5. Include frequent check-outs to ensure accuracy of hearing.

The summarization skill may be helpful to:

1. Begin an interview ("You said you wanted to see me about _____." "In our last session we talked about _____.").

2. Clarify what is happening, particularly when the interview is complex ("Could we stop for a moment and see where we are to this point?").

3. Provide smooth flow from topic to topic during the interview ("So far you've been saying_____. Now what's on your mind?").

4. Bring together what has been happening in the interview over the entire period of an interview ("Today, we talked about___").

5. Bring together threads of data over several interviews ("Last week you said_____and today you say___").

TRANSCRIPT OF SUMMARIZATION IN ACTION

You will now examine an interview which demonstrates summarization. Ordinarily, one does not summarize as frequently as illustrated in this example, but when you have a highly verbal client, you will find it helps both you and the client to summarize frequently. Otherwise you may become confused by the client's complex message. You will also find that good summaries help stop the client from saying the same thing over and over again.

The following interview is from the second session. You will find that the counselor is very active and is constantly bringing data together in summaries as she challenges the client to respect what she, the client, really wants.

Again, classify the counselor's leads with O?, C?, E, P, RF, and S. Give special attention to the check-out (CO). (Classifications may be found on page 105). In the counselor's leads below, give special attention to distinguishing between a combined reflection of feeling/paraphrase and the summarization. Recall that the summarization covers several statements and longer period of time. (See the end of this chapter for skill classifications.)

---

1. Counselor: Susan, in the last time we were talking, I recall you talked about being a single parent, that requires organizing your time, requires you having an MBA in finance . . . *(Classify this statement and #3 together. They represent a single skill.)*

2. Client: Oh, yes, for sure.

___3. Counselor: ...have an enormous responsibility in raising children, and knowing what that means. In addition, you're fortunate enough to have a career so that's a career and a personal life. And you're saying, how do I get all that together. And I'd like you to sort of focus on what you want to talk about this afternoon.

4. Client: I guess I would like to talk about my career. I've been feeling like I haven't been going anyplace; like I'm at a standstill. You know I went on in the midst of a separation and divorce and did get a masters' degree in counseling and I've done a lot of work in the area. I've done some consulting and some workshops; and I seem to be able to do it right within the school system, you know, I don't venture out too far. I've been reasonably successful; but I just can't seem to make that break from moving from teaching into something else, into counseling or perhaps into business. I'm trained to work in the area, but somehow I'm kind of afraid to move.

___5. Counselor: So, on one hand here, you are feeling good that you've accomplished all this, getting your degree, and you ought to be moving forward and doing something different; and on the other hand, it's fairly comfortable sitting where you are with the present job you've got. Have I got that straight?

6. Client: Yes, it's very comfortable. I like the people I'm working with and the schedule; it matches my children's schedule. I have the same holidays they do, and the same summer vacations; and

when you're a single parent, that's important. I can be with them and help them with their activities and homework and all those kinds of things. I'm kind of afraid though if I move away from education and go into business, I would be much busier. You know, it would be eight to five and weekends perhaps and two weeks vacation. That's a big change for me, from teaching.

___ 7. Counselor: Well, are you saying that if you leave the school system, the responsibility of taking care of your children is such that you can't take on the responsibility of a new job? And that it's probably going to be more demanding. *(Note, the question mark after "job?" does not indicate a question. Rather, helpers often raise the tone of their voice at the end of a paraphrase, reflection of feeling, or summarization with an implied question. This questioning tone functions much like a check-out, but is not classified. Do not confuse questions with a questioning tone of voice.)*

8. Client: Well, I'm kind of worried about whether or not I can handle all that responsibility. I can barely hold it together as it is now. But finance is tied in there too, Jane, because as you know, education is not the place to be these days. I mean, you don't make a lot of money when you're working in school systems; and I would be able to make more money if I moved out and did some things in business. But, you know, it's like . . . you know, the trade-offs are there all the time. I just don't know if I can hack it.

___ 9. Counselor: So, in other words, there are the successes that you've had in your career, the success that you've had in bringing up your children, suddenly the . . . really the heavy burden of finances is getting more so with the economy where it is now. And now you're faced at a point where you want or have to make a change.

_____ And what's going to happen to make that change?

10. Client: Yes...Well I think it might be an upheaval for my kids and for myself. . . it will be a whole change in our lifestyle and things have been going fairly smoothly, and fairly successfully, and you know, I'm afraid to rock the boat. Yet, on the other hand, I'd like to try some new things.

_____ 11. Counselor: Let me throw something out to you. If you were a man, and faced with this dilemma, what do you think would happen?

12. Client: Well, I think men are trained to move up the hierarchy just a little bit easier. I mean, they just take those risks and they move up, and I think women, you know, aren't trained that way. We're looked to be successful if we raise our kids and the kids turn out pretty well and if we hold a reasonably competent job, then we look pretty successful. And I don't know.

_____ 13. Counselor: I hear you talking about women, but are you describing yourself? *(The client has talked in general terms about women The counselor asks her to focus on herself.)*

14. Client: Yes, I think right now I look pretty successful in the eyes of a lot of other women and a lot of my friends. And I'm not sure I'd find that same success out in the business world.

_____ 15. Counselor: So, there is something in the fear of a failure at this point?

(Again, the questioning tone of voice.)

16. Client: Right, a fear of failure, and not being so successful.

_____ 17. Counselor: Susan, let's go back to what does success mean to you?

18. Client: Well, I think it is important that my kids turn out well; and that is very important. I'm very proud of their accomplishments so far. I think it's important to be personally satisfied, perhaps satisfied in a career. It's important to be financially independent or responsible enough that I can manage things without too much difficulty; and of course, that's a big thing right now. I also would like to, you know, just push myself a little more. Push myself to those limits and see what those limits are. That sort of gets in the way of all these other things.

____ **19. Counselor:** Let me summarize again. One, it's important for you to be a good parent, the other, it's important for you to have a career, the other, it's important... the economics is important. But there's another thing that I heard, that maybe you'd like to push yourself. You know, maybe take a chance. And maybe you think that . . . or maybe it would be helpful for us, for you to focus on maybe yourself, personally, and not that the others aren't important, but why don't we focus on you, Susan, and where you're going to go?

20. Client: What I'm going to do with my life, you mean?

____ **21. Counselor:** Several times, Susan, I've asked what you want. You seem to focus on other's needs and seem to find it very hard to speak about what you want. One of the things that I'm picking up is that you're not willing or anxious to look at what you really want even though we are talking about it right now. You really don't feel it's time to think of just Susan. Am I hearing you correctly?

22. Client: I'm afraid you're right. I guess I don't.

____ **23. Counselor:** You're afraid I'm right.

24. Client: You know it's hard for me to get an image of what I would be beyond what I'm doing now.. Well, maybe, you know, having a job with more responsibility, being in contact with more adults, maybe doing some supervision. It's real hard for me to get a handle on that. I don't know. I don't see any models out there of what I want to be like. I've seen a lot of models of what I'm like right now, but I don't see the other. It's very hard to imagine it.

_____25. Counselor: It's hard to imagine. So far, I'm hearing very much that you'd like to move on and use your masters degree in counseling—most likely in business. I hear that you feel good about what you've done professionally and personally. And I hear you struggling now with the desire to move toward some action. Am I hearing you right?

26. Client: Exactly, I think I need to talk more precisely about getting out and looking for a new job. It sounds like I'm spinning my wheels again and again.

You will often work with clients who present diffuse, confused thinking on complex topics. They need help in organizing the major issues and clarifying their thinking. The example above is fairly representative of verbal clients who are trying to take many factors into account in making a decision. You will also work with less verbal clients who have even more complex decisions to make. Here again, the ability to summarize and bring data together is a most important skill.

SUMMARIZATION WITH FAMILIES AND GROUPS

In some ways, the summarization skill is even more important in group and family counseling. Not only do you need to summarize what occurs with each individual, you also need to be able to summarize the many complex interactions of the family or group. Some might argue that the summarization skill is second in importance only to questioning skills when you work with groups. Certainly, summarization is a skill which can help groups and families build better understanding and more harmonious relationships.

The following are some specific types of summarizations which can be useful in group and family interviewing.

1. *Beginning or ending an interview.* It is especially helpful to a group if the helper summarizes where they were in the last session or what happened during a session. This provides you with an opportunity to include everyone, make observations on group interaction, and highlight important issues.

2. *Summarizing sequences of conversation or behavior.* Often you will see a family or group in which certain people speak first and then others either agree or disagree in a continuing sequence. It helps a group to look at itself when you point out, for example, "Father just reprimanded Jane. This was followed by Mother comforting Jane and by Bob moving closer to his Dad. I've seen this pattern several times today. What do you make of it?"

3. *Summarizing diverse points of view or issues of conflict.* You can be on the spot in family counseling or in group sessions. If you summarize what each person has said, you have shown ability to hear everyone equally. This supports each group member, gives you some neutrality in complex situations, and helps the group look at its own process.

4. *Summarizing group process.* A major distinction between individual and group/family work is a focus on what is happening among members. Almost any type of summarization in which the words "family" or "group" are used instead of individual observations represent this type of summarization. For example:

This group has a pattern of starting slowly.

This seems to be a family which is careful of protecting its members.

This group seems to enjoy conflict.

This family needs to need conflict to hold it together.

Each of these summary statements needs to be amplified by examples, but at times, the one-line summary above will produce considerable action and reaction in the family or group.

PRACTICING SUMMARIZATION

1. *Develop a working group.*

2. *Assign roles* as helper, helpee, operator/observer, and second observer.

3. *Determine topic for role-play.* A very useful topic is your own vocational future and the decisions you need to make around it. Almost any decision you have to make which involves multiple dimensions, however, is appropriate.

4. *Task of the interviewer.* Begin the interview with an open question, use some paraphrases and other skills to bring out data, and then summarize what the role-played client says periodically; and be sure to end the practice interview with a check-out.

5. *Watch time carefully and provide feedback.*

6. *Rotate roles.*

GROUP/FAMILY PRACTICE IN SUMMARIZATION

It is suggested that couple counseling be tried for this practice session. A family or group session could be attempted but will involve a fairly long time for adequate problem development.

1. *Develop a working group.*

    a. Two members become the couple

    b. Helper

    c. Observer/recorder

2. *Determine topic for role-play.* Any type of couple conflict is appropriate for this practice session. The practice session will likely be more effective if the couple has a difference of opinion about an important decision—moving to a new job, having a child, making an important purchase, where to spend

vacation, or how to spend money. Many couple problems occur in the process of making decisions.

3. *Planning.* The helper's task is to draw out the couple's conflict with as much information as possible. Ideally, the helper will want to know the facts of the situation as seen by each member of the couple, the feelings each has, and any reasons the couple can generate to explain what is occurring. The task is to draw out data and information, not to problem-solve.

Particularly important for the helper is to summarize the conflicting points of view accurately so that each member of the couple feels heard. In addition, the helper should attempt to summarize the interaction of the couple and patterns which may be observed.

During planning time, the role-played couple can generate a tentative "script" concerning their "difficulties." The observer can study the observer form and prepare any recording equipment.

4. *Watch time carefully and provide feedback.* The role-play should last approximately 10-15 minutes. Allow 15-20 minutes for feedback.

5. *Rotate roles as time permits.*

SUMMARIZATION

CLASSIFYING AND RATING SKILLS FOR QUALITY

As you view videotapes, listen to your own audiotapes, or watch a film, practice classify the leads of the helper as O?,C?,E,P,RF, and S. Use "Other" for skills that are other than those which you have practiced. To facilitate interview recall, write the main words of each helper response.

In addition, rate individual responses and the total interview on the following scale indicating your quality rating of the statement.

5 extremely helpful Use of skills greatly adds to and enriches communication
4 very helpful Use of skills adds to and enriches communication
3 helpful Use of skills adds slightly to communication
2 less helpful Use of skills detracts from communication (Frequent daily interpersonal interaction)
1 destructive Use of skills disrupts and significantly hinders communication

Skill—Quality *KEY WORDS OF HELPER STATEMENTS*

____ ____ 1. _____

____ ____ 2. _____

____ ____ 3. _____

____ ____ 4. _____

____ ____ 5. _____

____ ____ 6. _____

____ ____ 7. _____

____ ____ 8. _____

____ ____ 9. _____

____ ____ 10. _____

____ ____ 11. _____

A DO-USE-TEACH CONTRACT

1. I did use summarization during the practice sessions (when where, and with what effect?):

    _____

    _____

2. You will find it helpful to practice summarization when you help others make important decisions. It may be helpful to make lists of positives and negatives of important decisions and use these written data as part of your summaries.

    I plan to use this new skill outside this session in the following manner:

    _____

    _____

3. You may want to think about how you could help train peer counselors or family members in listening skills and how the skill of summarization fits into your plans.

    My plans to teach this important skill to someone else are as follows:

    _____

    _____

3. S 5. /P and CO 7. P 9. S —O? 11. O? 13. P/O? 15. P 17. O? 19. S 21. S—C) 23. E 25. S—CO

*Integrating microcounseling skills
into a meaningful whole is
accomplished through the five
stages of the interview.*

*Can you complete a full session
using only listening skills?*

CHAPTER 7

INTEGRATION OF SKILLS:
STRUCTURING AN EFFECTIVE INTERVIEW

It is possible to conduct a complete and successful interview using only listening skills. The foundation skills of attending are basic to effective interviewing and the information in this book will often be enough to enable clients to solve problems and to change their behavior, thoughts, and feelings.

Why are the listening skills so important? We believe the first task of the helper is to understand the helpee's point of view, feelings, and concepts. If we will listen carefully to others, we can help them understand their problems and opportunities. Many times they can make their own decisions and solve their own problems if we listen effectively.

We suggest that if attending skills are not sufficient, then it may be time to move on to skills of interpersonal influence. A companion book *Basic Influencing Skills* discusses skills such as interpretation, self-disclosure, and feedback. Yet, even as you move to more action in the interview, the basic skills of attending and effective listening remain central.

The exercises and readings in this chapter seek to help you:

1. Understand some problems and opportunities in the single skills approach to learning utilized in this book. You will be introduced to the "millipede effect."

2. Review the skills of this book as they are integrated in the *basic listening sequence.*

3. Define the structure of an effective interview.

4. Demonstrate that you can integrate the several listening skills in a full practice interview. You will also be encouraged to apply this framework in group and family sessions.

5. Use the structure of the interview in your daily life and in your own helping practice. Finally, we hope that you will consider teaching this structure to others as a way to improve their communication skills.

THE MILLIPEDE EFFECT

A millipede was walking happily along on a sunny day on its thousand legs. A fly flew by overhead and commented—"You certainly are clever millipede. How on earth do you coordinate all those legs."

The millipede responded, "Fly, I never thought of it before. I guess I just do it," and the fly buzzed off.

The millipede started to think, "The fly raises a good question. Now, do I alternate each leg down the line? Or do my left legs all go together and then the right? Just what do I do?"

The millipede collapsed and fell in the ditch. In the middle of all this thinking, the millipede's natural coordinated movement was disturbed.

Moral: *If you think too much about what you are doing, you may fall apart.*

The single microskills approach of this book has asked you to examine something you've done all your life without thinking about it. We naturally learn how to communicate, and you may have found a temporary decrease in your skills when you focused on specific dimensions. That is a natural part of learning.

Perhaps you took piano lessons or ballet. There you must work on single skills. You learn the importance of pulling out scales or specific body movements and practicing them to perfection.

The same principles apply in tennis, basketball, golf, skiing, and other sports. The person with natural ability can improve at music, ballet, or sports if he or she is willing to take time out to practice single dimensions and truly master them. But, when single skills are first practiced, there is a temporary decrease in performance and natural flow. Ultimately, natural abilities are improved by practice of important basic skills; and the skills become integrated in the person.

And, this is so with *Basic Attending Skills.* When you think about and practice the skills for the first few times, expect some decrease in performance. But, if you continue your efforts with the skills, you will find a new level of expertise, often far beyond your original level. The skills will become integrated into your own natural style.

An important maxim for you to recall:

Skill practice may result in a temporary decrease in communication. However, if you work on the skills and learn them to near-perfection, they will become a natural part of you ;and you may find yourself a greatly improved communicator.

THE BASIC LISTENING SEQUENCE: BASIC SKILL #7

You have practiced six specific skills with clients. All are based on a foundation of culturally appropriate attending behavior (eye contact, body language, vocal qualities, and verbal following). The next five skills are classified by their verbal structure: open invitation to talk, minimal encourage, paraphrase, reflection of feeling, and summarizations. In addition to these skills, the check-out has been stressed as an important addition to your listening skills to help clients respond more fully.

The basic listening sequence (BLS) is a way to integrate all the skills of this book in one useful package. The BLS was discovered while observing a manager at Digital Computer Corporation. An employee came up to the manager with a problem on the production line. The manager engaged in good attending behavior and responded to the employee as follows:

"Could you tell me about the problem on the production line?" *(open question)*

"You say the supply department hasn't given you enough computer chips to keep your group moving smoothly." *(paraphrase)*

"Sounds like the situation really makes you angry." *(reflection of feeling)*

The manager then *summarized* the employee's view of the problem and only then did he start to move toward action. *Encourages* were used to facilitate exploration on some key words of the employee.

As you can see, the BLS is an excellent way to summarize and integrate the concepts of this book. Not only are the concepts useful in management, but they are equally vital in the helping process. Counseling and psychotherapy can be said to be founded on the basic listening sequence.

The BLS also reminds us that we need to draw out the *facts* of the situation or problem and how the client *feels* about those facts. We can get this information through encouraging, questioning, paraphrasing and reflection of feeling. We also need to note how the client *organizes* these facts and feeling. It is here that the summarization is so helpful to both you and the client.

It may be helpful for you to think about the BLS and the specific listening goals of drawing out the facts, feelings, and organization of your client's problems and issues. Interestingly, many times the sequence of questioning, encourage, paraphrasing, reflection of feeling, and summarization can be followed in systematic order. It is not recommended, however, that you follow the BLS order all the time; but knowledge of the BLS and the importance of facts, feelings, and organization should help you in a multitude of helping, counseling, and therapeutic situations.

THE FIVE-STAGE INTERVIEW STRUCTURE: BASIC SKILL #8

Interviews can be structured in many ways, but one effective framework consists of five stages. If you learn this one model, you can adapt it with many clients with widely varying issues and concerns. You will also find it useful in situations where you work with a person who is culturally different from you, but again it will have to be adapted to the unique person before you.

In outline form the structure appears as follows. Note that the basic listening sequence (BLS) is used again and again in this framework. As you examine the five-stage structure of the interview, keep in mind that it should serve as a check-list, a framework which you can shape to meet the needs of each individual with whom you work.

Definition of Stage	Goals in This Stage	Skills and Multicultural Issues at Stage
1. *Rapport and structuring.* "Hello. Let me tell you what we will do in this session."	Develop a working relationship with your client. Share with your client how the session will be structured and its general purpose. Some personal sharing about yourself may be needed with some clients culturally different from you or are hesitant.	Culturally and individually appropriate attending behavior is the most important skill at this stage. You will want to generate an atmosphere of trust. With some clients that may take much longer than with others.
2. *Gathering information, defining the problem, and identifying assets.* "How can I help?" "What are some of your strengths?"	Obtain a clear summary of the client's problem. You will want to know the critical facts, feelings, and organization of the problem. Also, focus on positive strengths of the client.	The BLS will be especially helpful in discovering relevant data. With some clients from some cultural background, it may be wise to work through the goals of Stage 3 first.
3. *Determining outcomes.* "What do you want to have happen?"	You don't know where you're going unless you have a goal. Interviews may be aimless unless you have a purpose for the client.	The BLS will be useful in drawing out client goals and how the client feels about and organizes these goals. A clear joint statement of goals can be especially useful when the client is different from you.
4. *Exploring alternatives and generating solutions.* "What are the possibilities?" "What are you going to do about ithe situation?"	Having clarified the goal and the problem, you can turn to brainstorming solutions, making lists of possibilities, and prioritizing possible actions. This phase of the interview is usually the longest.	Again, the BLS will be critical. You will find that clients can often generate their own ideas if you use skillful questioning and encouraging. If the client misses obvious possibilities, you may at this point want to turn to influencing skills. Some clients, both culturally different and similar to you may want or demand your advice.
5. *Generalization and* transfer of learning. "Are you really going to do something about it?"	This is the phase of the interview which is most often forgotten. It is important to contract with your client to ensure that they act on learnings from the session.	Again, the BLS will be useful in working with your client to determine some future action. You may need to share the reasons for follow-up.

EXTENDING THE FIVE-STAGE INTERVIEW TO OTHER CONTEXTS

Although it was designed originally for full interviews, it is possible to use the five-stage structure of the interview in short contacts with helpees and even friends and family members who seek advice. When you are short of time and need to make contact with a client, recall the five stages as a checklist:

1. Do you spend some time in the contact on rapport and relationship? Time spent in developing personal relationships pays large dividends over time.

2. Do you draw out the facts, feelings, and organization of the client's problem? If you focus just on one dimension, you may lose valuable data.

3. Do you and the other person have a goal in mind or are you "just talking?" "If you don't know where you are going, you may end up somewhere else."

4. Do you allow the other person to generate ideas on their own before you give them your suggestions or advice? If you listen to their concerns first, they may solve the issues on their own.

5. Do you suggest specific follow-up actions so that new and useful ideas are tested rather than forgotten?

When it comes to using the five-stage structure, you will have a large number of possibilities in your daily life outside of the interview.

USING THE FIVE STAGES WITH LESS VERBAL CLIENTS

In Chapter 3, suggestions are given for helping hesitant or less verbal clients in the interview. The importance of questions requiring shorter, concrete answers was mentioned. You will find those pages helpful in adapting the five-stage structure with less verbal clients.

At the rapport stage, for example, your own conversation should be concrete and clear with a minimum of abstract concepts. It can be helpful if you share a concrete experience of yours early-on in the interview. If you stay at the concrete level, you will find that meanings between you and the client are more easily shared.

Misunderstandings can arise when counselors talk in intellectualized, abstract language.

In defining the problem, search for specific examples. Be willing to listen to concrete, detailed stories from your clients. In that way, they can express themselves more clearly. In establishing goals, focus on items which are very specific and observable. An abstract goal would be "I want to get along with my family better" whereas a concrete goal would be "To get along with my family, I am going to start doing specific things (for example, list playing games, helping around the house) with them."

Brainstorming alternatives at the problem-solving stage can be a problem for the less verbal client. Help the client concretize their goals and ways to reach their aims by asking specific questions which can be answered relatively briefly. Rather than generate five alternative solutions quickly, focus on each one by itself and discuss it concretely in more detail before moving on.

For both verbal and less verbal clients, making very concrete plans for generalization and taking new learnings from the interview is important. Specify changes in behavior as concretely as possible indicating with whom, at what time, and in what place attempts to change will take place.

With children and adolescents, the suggestions above may be useful. As mentioned previously, younger children can talk more easily if they have toys, games, or art to use while they talk to you. Adolescents are often edgy and full of energy—it may be useful to have objects available for them to touch as they talk with you (but only if you have the ability to be patient with their "fiddling." With many adolescents, it may be better to go out and play basketball, table tennis, or go for a walk rather than requiring them to sit quietly in your office.

STRUCTURING THE INTERVIEW WITH FAMILIES AND GROUPS

You will find that families and groups do not follow the five stages as easily as do individuals. The diversity of interests and needs may lead to some people in the group being at the first rapport stage while someone else is ready to start brainstorming solutions.

Basic Attending Skills is not designed to make you an expert in group counseling. Nonetheless, you will find the foundation concepts helpful in dealing with both unstructured and structured groups.

Unstructured Groups

Group counseling usually occurs over several sessions with ten three-hour sessions being a common length. Those expert in group process note that unstructured groups (encounter, marathon, or "T-groups") often go through stages themselves which may or may not agree or be workable with the five stages discussed here. Many unstructured groups go through some variation of the following:

> *Forming.* During the first stages of a group, particularly those which are unstructured or stranger groups, you will often find polite social inter-action. However, the lack of leadership eventually leads to frustration. Attending skills and observations of group nonverbal behavior on the part of the leader may be useful here.
>
> This group stage is parallel to the rapport/structuring phase of the interview as people are trying to know one another and find a structure for the group.
>
> *Storming.* During the next stages of a group, particularly those which are unstructured or stranger groups, you will find considerable frustration as the group attempts to find itself and its direction. There is often a struggle for leadership and power. Your leadership skills of para-phrasing, reflection of feeling, and summarization are often useful here. The influencing skill of feedback may be particularly important—here the leader gives accurate feedback on what he or she observes in the group Note the focus of leader comments is often on the grou*p as a whole* rather than on single individuals—"This *group* seems very angry right now."
>
> In some ways storming is similar to the second stage of the five stages of the interview. The problem which the group wishes to work on may be defined, at least in preliminary form.

Norming. The group starts to settle down at this phase. Members share themselves more freely. A cohesiveness develops which makes problem definition and goal setting possible. Norming corresponds closely to stages 2 and 3 of the five-stage interview. Problems and group goals may be defined here.

The group members start working on their own interaction or on a joint problem. Norms and ways of interacting have been established and the leader can continue using the same skills as outlined earlier. If you have modeled effective listening and feedback, group members themselves may start using these same skills more effectively. *Your importance as a model of effective communication cannot be overstressed.*

Performing. This is the work stage of the group. Individuals may test out new behaviors. Disagreements may be worked out more constructively. Your focus on the group as a whole may pay important dividends here. Groups members may start to look at themselves and how they relate to the total group process.

Again, your ability to listen and provide feedback is important. You may help the group and specific individuals examine how their behavior in the outside world is similar to their behavior in the here and now of the group.

Terminating/adjourning. As a group comes to the end, you will find that many of the old issues between members reappear and need to be worked through once again. The sense of loss when a group ends can be a problem for some members and old separation anxieties are brought out. The skills of summarization and reflection of feeling may be particularly important in helping a group work through this stage.

Unstructured groups can benefit from the concrete structuring of generalization offered within the five-stage interview. If each member can contract for a specific change or follow-up, the chances of long-term benefit from the group experience are greatly enhanced.

The listening skills emphasized in this book are important starting points for group and family work. As you develop more knowledge and expertise in the helping field, you'll find the information presented here on listening remains foundational.

Structured Groups

Structured groups also tend to meet with a defined period of time. The major distinction is that the topic is agreed to before the group starts. You may find yourself leading a group of high school or elementary students exploring their common concerns over family alcoholism or divorce. You may conduct a structured group in consciousness-raising for women, minorities, the developmentally challenged, or gays/lesbians. You may start a self-help group for cancer victims, families of Alzheimer's patients, or business people who have just lost their jobs.

You will find that the forming, storming, norming, performing, and adjourning concepts discussed above will also be a part of your work with structured groups; but usually, the interactions are less pronounced as the group members often had specific goals as they joined. However, the surprise personal discoveries in a structured group often require you to use many of the same behaviors and leadership styles of the unstructured group process.

In structured groups, the five stages of the interview may be followed more closely, but you will find that entire sessions may focus on any one stage. For example, the entire first three-hour session is likely to focus on rapport building and learning how a particular group is to be structured. You will seldom, if ever, actually go through the entire five stages of the well-formed interview when working with a group.

Throughout this book, we have stressed that it is important to use the listening skills in much the same way as you might use them when conducting individual sessions. We have also stressed that it is important to focus on the group as a whole. ("This group is anxious right now—everyone seems to want to avoid the pain and fear of the possibility of a cancer recurrence." "This group seems to be telling self-defeating stories—there are people who have learned how to grow beyond alcoholism.")

We have suggested in working with structured groups that you give one-third of your time to the group topic (cancer, divorce, eating problems, racism, sexism), one-third of the time to personal thoughts and feelings around the topic, and one-third of the time to group process—how the group itself deals with the topic.

You will find that you can use attending behavior and the skills of the basic listening sequence as your basic skill framework for much of your work with groups.

Family Sessions

Family counseling and therapy may be the most complex and difficult helping framework. Families move rapidly between forming, storming, norming, performing, and terminating sometimes all in one interview. Families often will want to focus on an individual when they need to look at their family interaction. And when, one individual needs attention, they may turn to discussing some other topic.

Your listening and attending skills will serve as good foundations for family work, but you will want to study much further before you attempt to work in depth with family counseling. If you are trained in individual counseling, you may be tempted to focus on individuals. In groupwork, it is important to focus on the word "group." In family work, you will need to use the word "family" again and again to help the individuals focus on their interactions rather than on a single family member.

In your role-plays and practice sessions, the five stages of the interview are workable frameworks for practice in family counseling:

1. *Rapport/structuring.* It is wise to spend time in a family session developing some sort of individual rapport with each member. At the same time you want to *join* the family as a temporary member; and this means seeing yourself as both a family member *and* as an observer.

2. *Problem definition.* Many families come to counseling with an "identified patient," perhaps the family alcoholic, the bulemic, or the acting-out child or adolescent. Many family therapists ask each member of the family to define the problem. They listen carefully and reflect back to each person what they have just said. Later the counselor often summarizes the varying family perspectives and reframes or reinterprets the individual issues as a family problem. *The focus moves from the individual to the family interaction itself.*

The problem definition phase is vital in family work, perhaps even more so than in individual counseling. You will be tempted to focus on single individuals and their problems. Family therapy stresses the importance of seeing any individual issue always in the context of family.

3. *Establishing goals.* A process very similar to the above occurs in setting up family goals. Each person has their say, and then the counselor helps the family establish joint family goals for more effective interaction. For example, instead of stopping an adolescent from acting-out, the goal of the family turns to becoming a family that works together more effectively.

4. *Exploring alternatives.* There are many theories and practices in family work which you will want to study and master. As you begin, your ability to listen will remain vital. If you listen effectively and focus on the family as a whole, often the family will being to generate their own solutions.

    Balancing your listening between family, individuals, and the topic (the family problem) will be helpful both as you begin and as you master family therapy. The counselor needs to balance focus on the agreed-on family topic (for example, how can this family work together more effectively and not be so focused on acting-out, bulemia, alcoholism, etc.), individual members thoughts and feelings, and on specific instances of family group interaction here and now in the session with the counselor which relate either to individual reactions or the agreed-upon topic.

5. *Generalization.* Families seem to benefit from concrete homework assignments so that they can take what they have learned in the group/family situation and apply it at home.

In summary, structured and unstructured groups and family sessions are indeed different from individual counseling and therapy. Yet, the skills you learn in individual work can be applied rather directly to groups and families. Again, it is important that you engage in further study and practice in these areas. The material here is designed as a brief introduction to some of the key concepts of work with more than one individual.

PRACTICE AND FOLLOW-UP WITH SKILL INTEGRATION

The task of this session is to demonstrate that you can conduct a full practice helping session using only attending and listening skills.

1. *Develop a working group.* To practice integration of skills, it will take more time. While groups of four are most desirable, it may be necessary to work in triads or pairs.

2. *Assign roles* as helper, helpee, operator/observer and second observer.

3. *Determine topic for role-play.* The five-stages of the interview are particularly effective in helping a client make a decision. Some useful decision topics include vocational choice, making a major purchase, deciding how to handle a specific interpersonal conflict, or your future as a professional helper.

   The following specific guidelines may be helpful for the role-played counselor:

   a. Rapport/structure. Spend necessary time tuning yourself in with the client in your own way and inform him or her of the purpose of the interview.

   b. Defining the problem. Use the BLS to draw out the client's issue. Be sure to spend some time defining client strengths. Remember that the concrete question, "Could you give me a specific example?" used in varying form will be useful in all stages of the interview to expand and clarify what is happening.

   c. Determining outcomes. Again, the BLS can be helpful in drawing out what the client sees as a goal or ideal outcome.

   d. Exploring alternatives and generating solutions. Begin this section by summarizing the problem and the outcomes as desired. Ask the open question, "Could you tell me what ideas/possibilities for resolution come to your mind?" You will find that the organization of the problem offered by the BLS and the five-stage structure often helps many clients find new and workable problem solutions here.

e. Generalization. Through attending skills and questioning, help your client define something specific he or she might do during the coming week to implement the ideas generated.

4. *Provide as much time as needed and provide feedback.*

5. *Rotate roles.*

GROUP/FAMILY PRACTICE IN STRUCTURING THE INTERVIEW

It is suggested that couple counseling be tried for this practice session. A group or family session could be attempted, but will involve a fairly long time for adequate discussion.

1. *Develop a working group.*

   a. Two members become the couple

   b. Helper

   c. Observer/recorder

2. *Determine topic for role-play.* Similar topics as those used for summarization are suggested. Any type of couple conflict is appropriate for this practice session. The practice session will likely be more effective if the couple has a difference of opinion about an important decision—moving to a new job, having a child, making an important purchase, where to spend vacation, or how to spend money. Many couple problems occur in the process of making decisions.

3. *Planning.* The helper's task is to draw out the couple's conflict with as much information as possible. Ideally, the helper will want to know the facts of the situation as seen by each member of the couple, the feelings each has, and any reasons the couple can generate to explain what is occurring. The task is to draw out data and information, not to problem-solve.

Particularly important for the helper is to summarize the conflicting points of view accurately so that each member of the couple feels heard. In addition, the helper should attempt to summarize the interaction of the couple and patterns which may be observed.

Use the same suggestions for structuring the interview as were summarized above for the individual session, but adapt the structure to meet the needs of the couple. You will find that the summarization skill is particularly important in couple, family, and group interviews.

During planning time, the role-played couple can generate a tentative "script" concerning their "difficulties." The observer can study the observer form and prepare any recording equipment.

4. *Watch time carefully and provide feedback.* The role-play should last approximately 10-15 minutes. Allow 15-20 minutes for feedback.

5. *Rotate roles as time permits.*

SKILL INTEGRATION FEEDBACK SHEET

Use the following form to classify the skills of the helper. Make a note on the form when a new stage of the interview begins. Classify the leads of the helper as O?,C?,E,P,RF, and S. Use "Other" for skills that are other than those which you have practiced. Write the main words of each helper response. In addition, rate individual responses and the total interview on the following five-point scale indicating your quality rating of the statement.

5 maximally facilitative — Use of skills greatly adds to and enriches communication

4 facilitative — Use of skills adds to and enriches communication

3 minimally facilitative — Use of skills adds slightly to communication

2 non-facilitative — Use of skills detracts from communication (Frequent daily interpersonal interaction)

1 destructive — Use of skills disrupts and significantly hinders communication

Skill—Quality   *KEY WORDS OF HELPER STATEMENTS*

____ ____ 1. _____

____ ____ 2. _____

____ ____ 3. _____

____ ____ 4. _____

____ ____ 5. _____

____ ____ 6. _____

____ ____ 7. _____

____ ____ 8. _____

____ ____ 9. _____

____ ____ 10. _____

____ ____ 11. _____

____ ____ 12. _____

*Continue on a separate sheet of paper using the same format.

Repeated below are suggestions for the five stages of the interview. Comment on the success of the interview in achieving the objectives of each stage.

1. Rapport/structure. Spend necessary time tuning yourself in with the client in your own way, and inform him or her of the purpose of the interview. How well was this objective achieved?

    _____

    _____

    _____

2. Defining the problem. Use the BLS to draw out the client's issue. Be sure to spend some time defining client strengths. Remember that the concrete question, "Could you give me a specific example?" used in varying form will be useful in all stages of the interview to expand and clarify what is happening. How well was this objective achieved?

    _____

    _____

    _____

3. Determining outcomes. Again, the BLS can be helpful in drawing out what the client sees as a goal or ideal outcome. How well was this objective achieved?

    _____

    _____

    _____

4. Exploring alternatives and generating solutions. Begin this section by summarizing the problem and the outcomes as desired. Ask the open question, "Could you tell me what ideas/possibilities for resolution come to your mind?" You will find that the organization of the problem offered by the BLS and the five-stage structure often helps many clients find new and workable problem solutions here. How well was this objective achieved?

_____

_____

_____

5. Generalization. Through attending skills and questioning, help your client define something specific he or she might do during the coming week to implement the ideas generated. How well was this objective achieved?

_____

_____

_____

DO-USE-TEACH CONTRACT

Your primary emphasis as you complete this book ideally will focus on the *use* dimension of the contract. How can you continue to use the skills you have acquired? How can you incorporate them into your daily life and in practical work in interviewing practice?

However, incorporating and truly making the skills of this workshop series part of yourself will take some time. It will require you to practice the skills deliberately. For these purposes the rating and count sheets used in this workshop can be most helpful. Copy them and use them as you examine your own interviewing style.

Whenever you have the opportunity—perhaps even tonight at home with your spouse or friend—audiotape or videotape a session. Analyze the interaction for yourself, and teach the other person how to analyze the session as well. Take a look at yourself at home and at work, and watch your helping style emerge.

What we are suggesting here is that you become your own teacher, your own advocate. Select the behaviors and skills you like, that seem to work for you. Change them, adapt them to make them your own. Ultimately, you must act alone. Perhaps by starting a simple process of self-observation you can maintain and continue your growth as a helper; and in this way you can come into closer touch with others.

Would you be willing to share one thing which you see as most important for you to follow up from this book?

_____

_____

How do you see yourself using the ideas of this book in the future? (Now, three months, one year?)

_____

_____

_____

Teaching helping skills to others is one effective treatment strategy.

This chapter shows you how to train individuals, families, small groups, and perhaps even community volunteers in these basic skills of personal communication and interviewing.

CHAPTER 8

TEACHING HELPING SKILLS TO OTHERS

This chapter is for the instructor and for those students who want to teach communication skills to others. Microcounseling is a scaled-down interviewing session in which a beginning counselor talks with a volunteer client about real problems. The interview occurs in a setting which provides interviewing practice with maximum opportunity for immediate feedback and trainee growth. The compressed nature of the situation allows a focus on specific dimensions of interviewing skills and does not demand that the trainee respond immediately as a fully professional counselor.

The central purpose of this book (and accompanying videotapes) is to provide helpers with a basic orientation to the skills approach to helping. By the end of each session, the beginning helper should have a specific understanding of a single skill and the ability to demonstrate that skill and classify specific behavior in an interview.

The extended objectives are defined in the "Do-Use-Teach Contracts." The effort here does not end with the teaching of skills in a classroom or workshop setting. We hope that people actually do use them and seriously consider teaching them to others—their clients, volunteer peer and entry-level helpers, and even professional colleagues. Our experience reveals that even many doctoral level professionals have more work to do on their basic skills.

Thus the objectives of the video and written materials are double—to teach specific skills and to provide methods by which those who have learned the skills can transmit them to others.

TEACHING AS TREATMENT

Basic Attending Skills is a foundation course in communication skills. We have found that teaching each of these skills to both outpatient and inpatient populations is a very effective adjunct to traditional counseling and therapy. Attending behavior and questioning skills are particularly helpful to clinically depressed clients. It is difficult to be depressed and focused on oneself when one is attending to someone else.

When you work with clients, many of them will have patterns of poor attending behavior. They may have poor eye contact or be unable to stay on the topic. Teaching the skills of attending can make a real difference in their daily lives. To teach skills such as attending behavior or questioning, recall the following framework:

1. Tell your client or patient what you are going to do and why. You are going to teach them a basic skill of communication which can make a real difference in how they relate to others. Many of your clients will have relationship problems. One route toward better social and family relationships is effective listening.

2. Define the skill clearly to them. Distressed clients may not be able to learn all four dimensions of attending behavior. If so, teach only one concept at a time.

3. Model the skill for them. Demonstrate poor listening and then demonstrate effective listening.

4. Have the client practice the skill with you in a role-play. The client may profit from demonstrating poor skills first and then more effective skills.

5. Assign homework to the client so that they practice the skills in their home settings.

A wide number of populations have benefited from learning communication skills. Groups as varying as parents and elementary children, convicts and priests, men who batter their families and women's consciousness-raising groups have all profited from learning these skills. Such skill training does not solve serious underlying problems, but does provide specific alternatives which can be part of problem solution.

Many of the clients who come to the counselor or therapist lack effective listening skills. You will find many individual clients, families, and groups that can learn about themselves and others through training in the Basic Attending Skills.

As a trainer, we urge you to consider helping your trainees learn how to teach skills either on a one-on-one basis or in small groups.

KEY ASPECTS OF THE TEACHING PROCESS

For what populations are the skill units designed? We have tried to write materials and design videotape mini-lectures and models so the classroom and training sessions and workshops may be suitable for a variety of people. Beginning helpers, teachers, parents, peer counselors, psychiatric aides, nurses, minority advocates, high school students represent only a sampling of the wide variety of populations with whom these ideas have proven successful.

Although the concepts can be used with a wide variety of trainee populations and cultural groups, it must be recognized that the examples and video models tend to represent primarily middle-class concepts and values. These materials, however, have been used successfully with a variety of trainees.

For example, Mary Bradford Ivey has adapted the concepts for teaching sixth grade children basic listening skills in a peer tutoring program. You may wish to adapt these materials and supplement them with specific examples more relevant to special group concerns.

With a more advanced group, for example, clinical psychology trainees, medical students, counselor educators, these same materials have been used success-fully. The vocabulary of the leader changes and adaptations of some exercises may be necessary. However, when working with such groups, the stress is on the *teaching role* of the professional. Advanced students appear to enjoy and benefit most from a workshop where they both learn skills for themselves and think about teaching helping skills to others. The professional helper is increasingly called upon to run workshops and train a wide variety of volunteer and lay populations.

How large a group can be taught using these materials? These workshops were planned for use with groups of approximately 20 people. However, the materials have been used with as few as one or two or with groups of up to 200 or more with appropriate adaptations.

A workshop could be managed with one leader and one videotape machine. The specificity of exercises and peer feedback gives virtually every participant a chance for significant experiential participation. Ideally, however, one leader for each 10-12 people is better. It is possible for the senior leader to train assistant leaders from the trainee population before the formal workshop.

What equipment is necessary? Ideal equipment would be a closed circuit video unit for each four people. This would ensure that everyone gets on tape several times. One unit for ten or twelve should permit each member to be on video once. Beyond that, it is best to recognize that not everyone can be on video and accept the fact that demonstrations are the only possibility with a small number actually seeing themselves. Thus a workshop could be run with only one T.V. unit.

The same workshops and class designs here can be run with no videotapes at all. Ideally, live demonstrations are used to present the skills in action. Student handbooks should be available for each participant. This provides a place for record keeping, a student log of the workshop, classification, and the do-use-teach contracts. It also gives the student something specific to take home as a product.

In addition, newsprint, masking tape, and felt markers are most useful and provide visual variety and interest.

The importance of practice. While we recommend videotape as the most effective medium, several researchers have found that verbal skills can be learned equally effectively using audiotape. We ourselves have found that simply telling people clearly and directly what is to be learned is often effective. Nonetheless, the multi-media approach of microcounseling with videotape appears to be the most enjoyable and successful method for involving people over a period of time.

Whether these tapes and materials are used in one-to-one counselor training or in workshop format, it is highly desirable that all participants have allotted time wherein they can practice videotaping counseling sessions outside of the immediate training situation. We have found that peer supervision is effective in supplementing formal microcounseling training.

THE BASIC MICROSKILL TRAINING FORMAT

Each workshop is structured with the following steps:

1.   *Warm-up/orientation.* The introductory pages of the chapter may be read. An elementary exercise may be used to warm up individuals for the workshop or training they are about to receive.

2.   *Reading.* Each chapter contains a short discussion of the basic skill. We suggest that the participants reread these brief manuals silently before viewing the videotape or seeing a live demonstration.

3.   *Viewing of video model or live demonstration.* Each skill is demonstrated so that participants can see the skill in action. If the videotape is not available, it is suggested that you as trainer do a live demonstration. You may want to make videotapes of yourself and different students for demonstration purposes.

4.   *Practice.* Specific suggestions for practicing each skill are included in each chapter. Go over these practice instructions with the trainees carefully in the early sessions of training. Then, when they have more experience, the groups will basically "run themselves." Note skill feedback sheets for each chapter.

5.   *Do-Use-Teach.* Some workshop leaders fail to use this portion of microtraining which helps ensure behavioral learning and retention.

6.   *Evaluation.* An evaluation form to obtain feedback about the chapter and your work as a leader are to be found at the end of this chapter.

Chapter 7, *Integration of Skills,* follows a somewhat more complex pattern and will be reviewed in more detail later.

Teaching Group and Family Skills. Each chapter has a section on adapting attending and listening skills for group and family practice. With beginning helpers, it is usually wise to skip this material, perhaps mentioning it briefly. But, as your trainees gain experience, they will want to attempt some of the group and family exercises.

Is it necessary to follow the precise ordering and procedures of these workshops? We firmly believe that each leader/trainer must adapt the suggested exercises to fit unique personality styles and situations. Those experienced in workshop development will want to change exercises and the order of activities almost immediately. Those just starting this type of workshop may want to follow the guidelines fairly precisely the first few times, but will later move to personal adaptations.

Our experience is that the general type of format presented here is usually quite successful with groups. It provides a reasonable balance of cognitive input with practice and time for people to practice and discuss issues. Nonetheless, each leader must be prepared to adapt materials as the workshop progresses. No one way is right. With experience, the "sense of the group" can be developed and exercises arranged to fit these needs as they appear.

How much time does it take to cover the materials in this book? With a tight schedule, it is possible to complete the six basic workshops in six two to three-hour sessions. It is preferable of course, to have more time. The shorter framework is effective when you have able, hard-working people who want to learn a maximum of information in a minimum of time. The problem with this intensive approach is that time for practice sessions is minimized and serious negotiation on the "do-use-teach" contracts becomes almost impossible.

Thus 20-40 hours is an appropriate time to cover the information provided here in depth while allowing for real mastery of the skills. Extra training time should be given primarily to providing individuals with a substantial amount of practice in the skills.

Originally we had suggested specific lengths of time for each exercise. We found through experience that some exercises can take ten minutes with one group and two hours with another. As such, the leader will have to select exercises and adapt them to fit the special needs and interests of each group.

Ethical questions. The workshop trainer should remember that we are working with people and usual standards for ethical conduct for training in counseling and group procedures hold. The *Microcounseling* text provides a discussion of ethical issues in microcounseling. Perhaps most important is the trainer being available to provide support and follow-up for any individuals who need or desire further counseling assistance.

At this point, it seems appropriate to turn to specific suggestions for teaching each chapter of the book.

TEACHING SUGGESTIONS FOR CHAPTER 2: ATTENDING BEHAVIOR

As this is the first training session, it is suggested that time first be spent in acquainting the group with one another. You will want to define the microtraining process as outlined in Chapter 1 so that your trainees are aware of the process.

The microtraining process may be summarized as follows:

1. *Warm-up/orientation.* Discuss the objectives of the first training session. Participants may want to share with the group or one another personal positive and negative experiences associated with listening and non-listening. A useful and humorous exercise is the demonstration "What Listening Is Not?" Summarize the group's or individual's observation.

2. *Reading.* Participants read or reread Basic Skill #1 on Attending Behavior and discuss its implications. Rapid readers may continue on to reread other parts of the chapter again. You may want to conduct a lecture/discussion to supplement the reading.

3. *Viewing of video or live model.* Show video model of the skill. Or, if unavailable, demonstrate the skill via live modeling.

4. *Practice.* Group instructions for practice are presented in detail in each chapter. If working with one individual, follow the same framework, but you will serve as the client and have to provide feedback. Stress the importance of written feedback using the feedback sheet.

5. *Do-Use-Teach.* Read through the ideas with your trainees, in pairs or groups of four, and have each person develop a written contract to take the ideas of the workshop out beyond the training session.

6.   *Evaluation.* Ask the participants to complete the evaluation form and turn them in to you. Permission to photocopy the evaluation form is granted.

TEACHING SUGGESTIONS FOR CHAPTERS 3-6

The format for each of these chapters remains the same as in Chapter 2. We have structured this third edition of *Basic Attending Skills* to simplify and clarify instructions. You will want to change format from time to time. Yet, it is our experience over literally hundreds of workshops, classes, and training sessions that the simple framework is always the best over the long run.

The basic framework is:

1)   Warm-up/orientation;

2)   Reading in the training session itself (it seems to develop better retention and learning);

3)   Viewing of video model (or live demonstration);

4)   Practice (have your students work toward mastery...going through the skills is not enough...can they make a difference in their clients?);

5)   Do-use-teach (the hardest part of the framework to maintain consistent use—develop a variety of ways to ensure transfer of training); and

6)   Evaluation. This framework works, produces results, seems to be interesting to students, is clear enough that students are able to use it themselves to teach others, provides a general model for teaching other skills and subject matter areas, and yet seems flexible enough to provide room for change.

Please recall that working with a single client or family with these skills can be helpful. This is especially true of attending behavior and questioning skills. If a person has the ability to listen to another person, this is an important start toward mental health and more effective personal relationships.

TEACHING SUGGESTIONS FOR CHAPTER 7

Given the structure of this chapter, it is likely that it will take you more than one session to complete the tasks suggested. The following order of exercises is suggested:

1. Divide into groups and provide time for get-acquainted or warm-up exercises as needed.

2. Read the Basic Skill summaries on the basic listening sequence and the five stages of the interview.

3. View the video modeling tape. Discuss the tape and the interview structure. If the tape is not available, discuss each phase of the session with your group.

4. The first time through, we have found it wise to have trainees work in pairs. Rather than go through an entire interview without stopping, we discuss each stage of the interview and have them practice that one phase. We stop after each stage for feedback. In this way, the stages are separated clearly and the objectives for each stage are achieved more easily. We have found that, in the early phases, trainees may move randomly from stage to stage unless the session is highly structured.

5. With the practice above as a background, we can then conduct a regular practice session with observers and feedback sheets.

6. Develop "Do-Use-Teach" contracts as indicated.

7. Evaluate the session(s).

The practice session for integration of skills and the five steps of the interview generally take longer than single skill practice. It is suggested that trainees repeat the process until they have mastered it to a high level. It is our belief that people should not move on to the influencing skills until they have thoroughly mastered the basic skills of the interview.

TEACHING HOW TO TEACH SKILLS

The Do-Use-Teach contract may be used as is. However, we prefer at this point to require our trainees to teach one another the skills of microtraining. We have found that this may be done even in a workshop setting using the following sequence:

1. Divide your group, regardless of size, into groups of four.

2. Two people in each group will select a skill that they would like to teach the other pair. The other two people select a skill they would like to teach to the first pair.

3. Planning time of about 30 minutes is allotted. During this time, the pairs plan a workshop consisting of: a) a warm-up exercise; b) reading this book coupled with some didactic presentation; c) live modeling of the skill; and d) supervised practice using feedback sheets.

4. The pair presents its skill workshop to the other pair.

5. The roles reverse.

We have found that an interesting teaching experience which reassures beginners that they actually can teach others counseling and communication skills is completed successfully in about two hours. Trainees are then prepared to go out and teach these skills beyond the workshops to parents, teachers, children, professionals, and a wide array of groups.

USING TRANSCRIPTS TO ENSURE TRAINEE MASTERY

An all-too-common tendency in counseling training is for the trainer to present information and assume that competency in the concept will develop. This is not necessarily so. We require students to practice skills and bring in tapes or transcripts weekly.

At the conclusion of training, our students present a complete interview typescript in which they demonstrate that they can conduct an interview using primarily attending skills, classify their skill usage, and discuss some of the implications of their work. The value of a typescript analysis is immense.

FEEDBACK FORM ON ATTENDING AND LISTENING SKILLS

Name _____ Skill area evaluated_____
(optional)

1. One thing in my behavior which I plan to change as a result of this session is:

2. One thing in my behavior which I want to continue and see as a strength is:

3. The most helpful incident in this training was:

4. If I were conducting this training, one thing I would add would be:

5. As follow-up, I am going to *use* the ideas from this workshop in this specific plan of action:

6. As follow-up, I am going to *teach* the ideas from this workshop to this specific group or person in this specific fashion:

7. Use reverse side of sheet for additional comments and/or suggestions.